Stealing Magnolias

TALES FROM A NEW ORLEANS COURTYARD

Debra Shriver

Preface by George Rodrigue
Foreword by Mary Randolph Carter

First published in the United States of America in 2010 by

Glitterati Incorporated
225 Central Park West, Suite 305
New York, New York 10024

www.GlitteratiIncorporated.com
Telephone: 212 362 9119
media@glitteratiincorporated.com for inquiries

First edition, 2010

Design: Sarah Morgan Karp/smk-design.com

Library of Congress Cataloging-in-Publication data is
available from the publisher.

Hardcover edition ISBN 13: 978-0-9823799-1-2

Printed & Bound in China
10 9 8 7 6 5 4 3 2 1

For Jerry

A Louisiana "welcome" greets New Orleans Jazz & Heritage Festival fans as they enter the Fair Grounds.

CONTENTS

The colors of Africa are captured in a necklace from JazzFest's Congo Square.

Creole shades of blue and green adorn a townhouse parlor.

PREFACE

George Rodrigue

It wasn't until 1989 that New Orleans became a place that I wanted to know better, a place that intrigued me as novel in its own right. That year I opened my gallery on Royal Street, and soon after I replaced the Cajun genre paintings in my window with paintings of the *loup-garou*, a ghostly werewolf based on a French story my mother told me as a child and, most significantly, pictured 'blue' in my imagination. During the 1990 Super Bowl I watched both tourists and news crews stop dead in their tracks as they passed my Royal Street Gallery window. The exposure made my paintings famous, and although I still painted and lived in Lafayette – where I had lived for the previous thirty years – it was in New Orleans that the *Blue Dog* was born.

Twenty years later, my wife and I call New Orleans home. We live in a Creole townhouse built in 1830 in a historic neighborhood called the Faubourg Marigny, a mere ten blocks from my gallery. In the evenings we sit on our porch and watch the tops of the ships, as they seemingly glide along the levee of the Mississippi River. We've learned that our house, built long before the levees, routinely flooded, with the water flowing through the first floor each spring. The house was a bar, a bordello, slum apartments, a party house for New Orleans' characters like Tennessee Williams, and an elegant tribute to historic preservation. In living here, we are a part of this history, and we enjoy the fact that we add to our house's narrative, and by extension to the story of New Orleans itself.

My wife and I moved to New Orleans ten years ago, but it's been a part of both our lives from the beginning. I grew up in New Iberia, Louisiana, a small Cajun town 130 miles west of the 'big city,' our destination for shopping and special family outings. Most memorable was our annual visit to Canal Street for the holidays, when we started the day with *beignets* at Café du Monde, followed by the Christmas decorations at D.H. Holmes, Maison Blanche, and Sears – my favorite because it had a giant Santa Claus.

The ubiquitous *Blue Dog*, a creation of painter George Rodrigue, poses before a Louisiana landscape.

In addition to the holidays, every few months we visited a distant relative, Cousin Marsolite. She lived on the first floor of a two-story house across the street from the old Pelican Minor League Baseball Field. I remember as a kid that during heavy rains her house flooded several inches, which must have happened often, since her furniture stood elevated on bricks, and as far as I know she kept it that way for the eighty years she lived in the house.

In 1967 I had moved to Lafayette, Louisiana, remaining for three decades and establishing myself as an artist of Louisiana landscapes and Cajun folk life. From this point New Orleans became a larger part of my life, a place not only suited to weekend getaways, but also to sell my paintings and further my career.

Unlike my hometown, New Orleans is not Cajun, and the people are completely different from those of us who grew up in the swamps along the Bayou Teche, just a two-hour drive away from the city. I spent more than twenty years trying to save through my art what I saw as my dying culture, something overtaken by the modern world, a world represented by (remarkably enough) a 300-year-old city. New Orleans' famous decadence, its railroads, and its ports along the Mississippi River both seduced and invited the outside world to exert its influences.

My wife thought of New Orleans in a different way. Her parents were born and raised on the West Bank (or 'across the river'). They married at the Algiers United Methodist Church and celebrated special occasions at the Blue Room at the Roosevelt Hotel. Her mother and grandmother, adorned in white gloves, hats, and their Sunday best, shopped on Canal Street in the 1950s, and her grandfather was a legend in the area's oil industry. For her, New Orleans is "home," because every day she retraces her roots and becomes a bigger part of something started long before her. It's where she belongs, and she thinks it nothing unusual to attend a psychic reading at the Bottom of the Cup Tea Room (est. 1929), or dressing in a wig and costume for her annual ride in the all-female Muses parade at Mardi Gras, or just window-shopping on Chartres Street, deftly traversing the chipped slate sidewalks in her stiletto heels.

In *Stealing Magnolias*, Deb Shriver shares *her* New Orleans love story, a continuing and fluid account of exploration and wonder. Whereas for me it was the *Blue Dog*, something rooted in Cajun folklore, developed and altered by New Orleans's influence, which sparked my passion for

Landing of the Rodrigue Brothers finds the *Blue Dogs* in a Cajun bayou as George Rodrigue explores Louisiana heritage.

this city; for Deb it is the magical and symbolic "Catching Coconuts." Like many of us, she learned that one never fully understands this place. Rather, it invites the locals to poke around corners and, well, play tourist. Just this year my wife and I purchased a building adjacent to St. Louis Cathedral where, after twenty years in the same rented location across the street, we moved my gallery. It's a milestone in my life and career, and yet the 200-year-old building sat right there, staring at me unnoticed and taunting me, for two decades.

I never imagined as a child that I would one day call New Orleans home, and yet after Hurricane Katrina, I could imagine living nowhere else. Water has flowed through this city forever, long before "the storm," and yet the original footprint remains intact; the old buildings change hands and fulfill dreams; and the people stay loyal to this place. Once it gets a hold, there is nowhere else to go. I relate to Deb Shriver's ongoing passion for this city, and like many locals, I understand the emotion and excitement she describes throughout this book, because in 2010, after all this time, New Orleans, through this incredible combination of art and narrative, has seduced me once again.

FOREWORD

Mary Randolph Carter

My husband bought me my wedding ring in a tiny antique shop on some now forgotten little street in the French Quarter. It was the first time I had been there and when we returned we were married. I should have been jealous of New Orleans for he fell in love with her as a young college student from New York City – way before he met me. Maybe the fact that I was born in Virginia, a Southern woman with too many names, rekindled in him something he felt he'd left behind. He would say, "No," that I have over-romanticized the whole thing, but what he can't deny is the spell that New Orleans still holds over him, now us, and how he/ we can't wait to get back. Debra Shriver describes it as *coup de foudre*, the French term for love at first sight, and that's what her *Stealing Magnolias* is all about – her *coup de foudre* for New Orleans and eventually for the old house with the leafy courtyard that she and her husband fell for on Dumaine Street . . . three weeks before Katrina hit.

Though she appears to float through the narrow streets of the *Vieux Carré*, Debra Shriver is not one of Anne Rice's beautiful vampires. Oh, no! She is very much alive, nourished by the sights and sounds and smells and tastes of the beauty and magic of a city that seduced her long ago. *Stealing Magnolias* is her, as she puts it "part-love story and part-scrapbook," filled with tales crafted from her words and the borrowed images of artists that share her vision of the Big Easy, the Un-Easy, her very own Un-forgettable New Orleans. She takes us along, and like a good friend unabashedly in love, shares every detail of her romance with her New Orleans and her journey of creating a second home and refuge from her other life in New York City. Here are her favorite streets, houses, peeling paint, gardens, flowers, scents, music, artists, foods, recipes and rituals like *lagniappe* (lan-yap!), a Creole word for "something extra" that she gives us in the form of her own address book. In the beginning of her tale is a quote by the wonderfully wry English writer, Roald Dahl: "Those who don't believe in magic will never find it." Believe in magic and you will find it in *Stealing Magnolias*. I did.

Antiques fill a showroom at Karla Katz and Co. on Magazine Street.

...ELEBRATES THE MARDI GRAS CARNIVAL WITH COLORFUL PARADES

...SE BEADS WERE GATHERED IN NEW ORLEANS
...AROUND THE WORLD AND RESTRUNG BY
THOMAS JAYNE AND RICK ELLIS.

...WERE DISPLAYED AT WINTERTHUR AS PART OF
...THEIR YULETIDE EXHIBIT IN A ROOM TITLED
"TWELFTH NIGHT IN NEW ORLEANS".

Mardi Gras

And above all, watch with glittering eyes the whole world around you because the greatest secrets are always hidden in the most unlikely places. Those who don't believe in magic will never find it.

—Roald Dahl

INTRODUCTION

The magic that is New Orleans found me long ago. This book is part-love letter and part-scrapbook. It contains my words, and the illustrations and photographs of a small band of gifted artists who share my devotion to this magical place. Between these covers are the images that draw me, an outsider, back to the city time and again. I am neither historian nor native daughter, yet I am bewitched. On these pages, I have compiled musings on the spell that New Orleans has cast upon me, the house my husband and I now call home, the foods we like to eat, the cocktails we often drink, the local music we listen to and play later to quell the home-sickness when we are far away, the jazz clubs and dive haunts we return to, the footpaths of grand gardens and homes we have visited, and the well-worn sidewalks of our neighborhood, the *Vieux Carré*. My efforts are impressionistic, and I am late with offerings. Still, New Orleans is always ripe for rediscovery. Bookshelves overflow with novels and history books dedicated to this city. Countless songs have been composed and sung. In fact, there are too many odes, and too many verses to remember. Writers continue to write about her, musicians continue to play and sing, and so, this is my verse and song, *my New Orleans.*

The author's collection of Mardi Gras beads gathered from around the world.

Catching Coconuts

I should begin with the morning I spent catching coconuts.

My husband and I had just returned home to New York City after an intoxicating week in New Orleans, our heads still spinning from the rush of Carnival madness. We veered from raucous parties and street parades to the wildly decorative fantasies of the fancy *bal masqués*, all of which led up to the crescendo of Mardi Gras. All it took was one friend, in this case, an editor strolling up Eighth Avenue, to ask about my trip, and I found myself reliving it all with the excitement of a child who had binged on too much candy. Except, in New Orleans, joy has a very 'old soul' quality. It is profound and complex and resonant. New Orleans is the place where you can be completely in the moment, yet still feel connected to every moment in the city's story that has led up to yours alone.

"So how was Mardi Gras?" my friend asked.

And so I began. I described the torch-lit procession by the plumed, masked 'dukes' of the Krewe of Hermes, enthralling the crowds atop their prancing stallions. Traditional flambé carriers marched ahead on foot, lighting their path through the nighttime revelers spilling along the parade route on Canal Street. Despite the chattering crowds, you could hear the crackling snap of the flames as they whipped and roared through the dark night sky. Their rustically-constructed torches were hoisted high, and provided a primitive element amidst all the formality and pageantry of the parading Hermes court.

I tried to recall for my friend the lavish finery worn by the fairy tale courts, the kings and queens of Carnival, with their gem-encrusted crowns, silver scepters and ermine-lined capes. Curtsying rows of fresh debutantes, virtually identical in their beauty, their pedigrees and their floor-length white ball gowns, donned white kid gloves and pearls (both in requisite opera length, *bien sur!*) A regular at such events described the scene as "serious make-believe." I told my New York friend how the court of King Comus, dressed head-to-toe in silver, bowed and nodded

Thousands of blue feathers and beads are sewn into a Mardi Gras Indian costume.

to the court of Rex, wrapped in elaborate folds of gold brocades and silks, during a regal ceremony that began an hour before midnight. They bowed and curtsied their way through formal presentations until both hands of the clock struck twelve, signaling the end of raucous Mardi Gras and the beginning of somber Lent.

I tried to paint a picture of the large *paper maché* head pieces worn by Comus Krewe members as they skipped and pranced before an elaborately painted tableau of European gardens. And I told him how every time I was 'called out' to dance at the various balls with yet another masked man in 18th Century costume, or a lovely white-gloved gentleman in white tie and tails (*costume de rigueur* read the invitation), each new partner had presented me with a small box afterwards. To my delight, each contained custom jewelry symbolizing the evening's theme – a bracelet charm in the shape of a small ship, a ribboned gold pendant fashioned like a French medallion, or a Napoleonic bee pin set in semi-precious stones.

"I can't even begin to describe it," I exclaimed to my editor friend.

I think that I may say that an American has not seen the United States until he has seen Mardi Gras in New Orleans.

—Mark Twain

Determined to drink in every Carnival experience (some of them literally), my husband and I awoke early on Mardi Gras morning. We enjoyed a breakfast of beer and street food – red beans and rice and a '*lagniappe*' (*New Orleanese* for 'extra') portion of fried chicken – all while standing at the intersection of Jackson Street and South Claiborne Avenue. There, we waited for the Zulu parade to begin, sandwiched among the rows of families from the neighborhood, some of them carrying small children on their shoulders – better to catch carnival beads, stuffed toys and Zulu coins tossed from passing floats. An hour before, we walked the mostly-African American neighborhood in Central City scanning the side streets for signs of parading, drum-beating Mardi Gras Indians. All wore full regalia: they were costumed, feathered, beaded and satin-draped to the nines as they grouped themselves to chant and pose for pictures. And then came the moment when New Orleans seduced me for life.

Carnival revelers dance in the street along St. Claude Avenue.

A festooned family of Mardi Gras Indians strike a pose during Fat Tuesday.

African-inspired masks cover face and totem during a Carnival celebration.
Opposite: A Venetian mask awaits its owner during a *bal masque*.

Some spells cast you into a moment of no return; New Orleans cast me into a moment of eternal belonging. As I jockeyed curbside for the perfect spot to view the Zulu parade, I scored the ultimate in Carnival prizes – a hand-painted, glittered coconut – the rarest, most sought-after parade 'throw' pitched into the throngs of Mardi Gras revelers. In their 'black face' and traditional Carnival dress of grass skirts and gold shoes, the Zulus threw me a symbolic key to their city and I caught it. Destiny was lobbed at me and I jumped to receive it.

Mardi Gras frames your concept of life in new ways. Later that evening, while strolling along St. Ann Street, I exchanged warm greetings with a good friend from New York City, an elegant gentleman, always sartorially turned out in bow tie and custom-made seersucker suit. Except, here in New Orleans, he was unrecognizable as he greeted me in drag. 'Carla' looked stylishly sultry in a pink wig, silver lame halter mini-dress and glittery six-inch knee-high platform boots.

These were the moments I took home with me, and tried to recount to my friend back on Eighth Avenue. He was speechless, then declared my experiences "surreal." Well, almost. "For most people, this would be a fantasy," he said. "For you, it's real life." And he was right. While I was dancing with masked strangers, searching for feathered Mardi Gras Indians, catching coconuts, then air-kissing my cross-dressing friend, nothing had seemed out of the ordinary. For me, it felt like the world was in perfect order.

A Dress Code for Debutantes

Beyond the strict Southern dictum of dress that has long existed – no hats after five o'clock, white shoes worn only between Good Friday and Labor Day, absolutely no velvet past Valentine's Day – there lives an unspoken dress code designed solely for the debutante set celebrating Carnival (known as Mardi Gras to non-natives). There are no written pronouncements, but unwavering rules are passed like heirloom china from generation to generation. Heaven help the out-of-towner, visiting Yank or tourist who get's it all wrong. The list is short but unerring, and is not altered by the passage of time or passing hemlines. For formal affairs, be it banquet or ball, the plain tuxedo pales in sartorial preference to white tie and tails (*de rigueur!*). For the fairer sex, toe-length gowns and white kid gloves (opera length *bien sur!*) rule the night, along with grandmother's jewelry, perhaps in the form of a single strand of long, lustrous pearls or a treasured brooch or bauble tastefully fastened at the waist, near the neckline or pinned upon coat, cape or clutch. Tiaras, unless you are Queen of the Court, are off limits, as are cocktail hats. A feather or ornament tucked into a twist of curls count as charming, and here, excess cleavage, either as *décolleté* or *derriere*, is *démodé*. As New Orleans social chronicler Diane Sustendal Labouisse puts it, "Carnival is a lot like church. Follow the lead of the ladies who are seated in the front rows as they are generally the family of the court and know the routine."

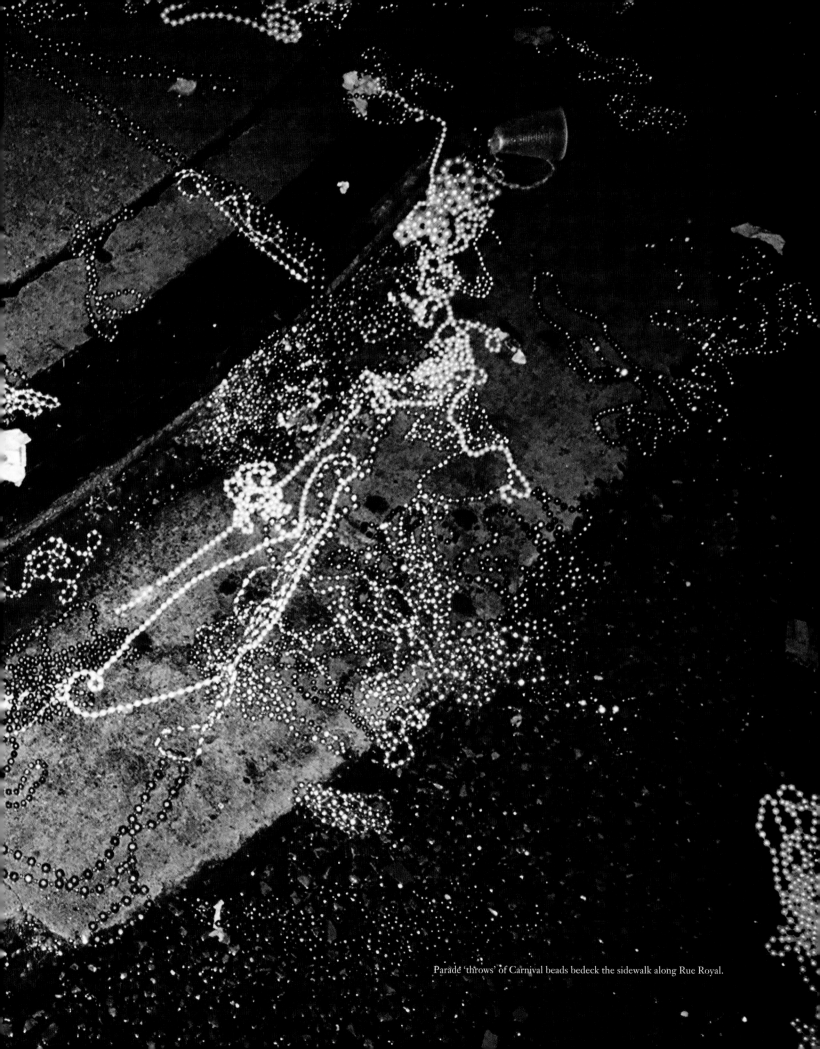

Parade 'throws' of Carnival beads bedeck the sidewalk along Rue Royal.

Coup de Foudre: The Spell is Cast

I am always dreaming of New Orleans, both in my sleeping 'travels,' and in my waking hours. Yet, with all my preoccupation with this three-hundred year old city, it is nearly impossible to isolate her, to try to break apart the elements of her magic. Locals call it her 'mojo,' a part-Creole, part-African word, now a slang term meaning magic by way of hoodoo or voodoo at play, or the casting of spells. The old city is at once exotic and familiar, cool and hot, scrappy and elegant, friendly and even dangerous. Her contradictions draw you in, and then, one by one, dominate your senses. Sight, sound, scent, and taste collude and conspire to captivate.

With each returning visit, I continue to pencil in the colors in my mind, to sketch her lines and angles, to try to define the magic. Is it the architecture from another time – with its alternating layers of grandeur and decay? Or what I like to call her 'invisible scenery' – the intoxicating elixir of bright sunshine mixed perfectly, like a Brennan's cocktail, with soothingly damp humidity and tropical heat that leaves you loose, languid and in a trance-like state. Is it the deep reverence and almost religious fixation with tradition and ritual? Or maybe it's simply the sheer intensity of appreciation for good times involving food, drink and revelry that is an antidote to the comparatively puritanical ways of those who live in the 'other' America.

A friend calls New Orleans 'Europe with heat.' She means the lusty, leisurely, European lifestyle is recalibrated to an even slower, heat-driven and tropical pace. Searing temperatures are matched only by the more palpable spices of its cuisine – a hot peppery jambalaya, the African-inspired ingredients of a salty *andouille* gumbo, or a spicy, roux-soaked *étouffée*. Neighborhoods, accents and menus are an irresistible mix inspired by France, Italy, a dose of Spain and the melding flavors of Africa, the Caribbean and the Deep South.

Scent rounds out the ambience, and like the French Quarter, never sleeps. The city's rich soil, continuous sunlight and high humidity create a greenhouse effect: magnolia, bougainvillea, sweet olive, night jasmine and its cousin, Confederate jasmine, perfume the air. Aromatherapy here is a walk through Jackson Square, or an outside table at the nearest café.

Decay greets the visitor to a French Quarter stairwell.

In a way, New Orleans is all about the moment of release, a deep, virtual sigh that surrenders all weight of thought and behavior, and slows the heart to a restful, rhythmic beat. Sound becomes the most prevalent, seductive element of all. The ease of 'The Big Easy' can be heard in a harmony of noises that recall it and nothing else, from the whisper of a dragonfly hovering above a clutch of magnolias, to the raucous blat of a trombone on Bourbon Street. All are ceaseless reminders to resident and tourist alike why it has been called "the most alive city on earth." Street musicians carrying saxophones, harmonicas and violins make their living playing throughout the French Quarter. I cross the sidewalk off Royal Street into Pirate's Alley, and hear a lone clarinet playing in the shade of St. Louis Cathedral. In the far distance, a young man stands on sun-parched, broken pavement, and blows into a trumpet as he scrunches his face into the mouthpiece and 'balloons' his cheeks, Louis Armstrong-style. A clanky-keyed piano bellows American blues out of a corner bar.

There is so much history and cultural richness in that city that it oozes up out of the sidewalk.

—John Scott

There are the sounds of trade and transport: ships and barges motor and puff through the river. Paddle wheelers blow that ancient whale-cry sound so often heard along the Mississippi, while their calliopes pipe pure Americana in John Philip Sousa's familiar refrains. Trains clack along the tracks. Horses clop. Cathedral bells mark the quarter hours. Voices of friends on the street mingle mid-air with those of strangers, rising in a *patois* of cadences and accents. Here, I detect a fast, guttural Brooklyn-ese with vowels that sound faintly Italian; there, traces of a French lilt even if the voice happens to be masculine.

New Orleans may be the only city with four or more distinct pronunciations of its name: the number of syllables change depending on the origin of the speaker. I sometimes hear locals, namely those living uptown, say 'New Or-le-ans' and 'Nyoo 'Ahhlyins'; and 'New Or-leens'

Photographer Josephine Sacabo's street musician pauses for an afternoon nap.

Two studies in chiaroscuro: a worn settee and a simple steel birdcage.

A banana plant morphs into a photographic diptyque. *Opposite:* Raymond Meeks' portrait of the remains of Windsor Plantation pays homage to an antebellum past.

by recent arrivals from elsewhere; and the touristy-give-away 'N'awlins' by those just passing through with their free city maps. Other cities refer to 'north' and 'south,' 'east' and 'west.' Here, the local directional language is 'upriver' and 'downriver,' 'lakeside' and 'north shore.' Locals like to describe its four main sections as 'uptown,' 'downtown,' 'back of town' and 'out of town.'

Each time I return to New Orleans, I become as spellbound as a first-time visitor. A few days here and my New York defenses fall. My breathing slows. The city's decay begins to feel romantic; the humidity soothing. The sunlight starts to draw me into its warm circle. Few, unlike me, escape her spell. The occasional visitor comes to town more frequently. The obsessed buys real estate.

Born under an astrological water sign, I have often thought that my lusty attraction to a city surrounded by water was some perverse version of a lunar fix – just me and the moon, locked in a close Zodiac embrace. Everything seems steeped in metaphor. I quaff glistening oysters in their briny liquid straight from their shells, and delight in the gathering clouds that pour their daily half-hour summer rainstorms onto our slate roof. I stroll the levees above Jackson Square on the edge of the French Quarter where the highest lip of soil stretches out to meet the horizon, which so perfectly frames the rolling Mississippi River. I swim in my own *aqua vitae*, for water is everywhere – in lake, river and gulf, falling from the sky, rising with the tide, but mostly, hanging in the air. This is the latitude and longitude that pinpoints the place where I feel most alive. Both the water and air mix in a way that awakens my coastal childhood memories. I think of the mythical siren call of 'the salt line,' the invisible divide from

Three studies from nature: thistle, magnolia bud and bananas.

It's a fragile and extraordinary patch of land that has served as the cradle of American architecture, food and music.

— Justin Lundgren

coastal plain to cypress swamp, about fifty miles inland from the Gulf of Mexico. Here, Native Americans and New World explorers came for the salt deposits, while sailors and river boaters heeded the tropical winds and the briny air. And Harvard professors talk about the primitive, gravitational pull of ancient lands and pockets of civilization espousing the 'four D's': dancing, drumming, drinking and decadence. Or perhaps, as one tourist put it, here, it's all about the 'three C's': Creoles, Cajuns and Catholics.

I not only love New Orleans; I love the idea of it. When I am away, it is a dream I can always return to. I would come just for the gumbo. Or for Mardi Gras. Or for the jazz. It is mystical and mysterious, and sometimes surreal. New Orleans is the place where I opened my front door on Twelfth Night to greet two old friends standing on the sidewalk dressed as the sun and the moon. It's where I look to the heavens, literally, to see the live oak trees on both sides of St. Charles Avenue spread their long limbs to create a canopy of leafy green foliage, high above the streetcar tracks. Once, I watched the mast of a ship float past a third-floor window in the Garden District, with no sight of the river. And, this was no mirage; just a ship sailing by in a city cached below sea-level. Here, the King of the Carnival Rex Krewe was once named 'King,' and city fathers are called 'Dutch' and 'Moon.' It's a place where a former mayor rests in an above-ground cemetery crypt alongside a legendary voodoo queen.

New Orleans is the birthplace of jazz, a music form whose songs, according to native son Louis Armstrong, are "never played the same way once." Substitute the word 'life' for 'jazz' and you begin to understand that both here are based on improvisation, collaboration, jubilation. No note of music, like no date on a calendar, will repeat itself. Life and jazz both are lived forcefully, mightily, in the present.

The swampy, oppressive climate combined with a tumultuous history pocked by fire, plague, battering hurricanes, floods and natural disasters, crime and at times, a heels-down economy, seems too much for a single city to absorb. New Orleans does wear her age, yet somehow is not yet jaded by time. She is flamboyant and bohemian and tropical. She is also 'Old World,' and grand and elegant still. No matter how heat, humidity and time try to ravage New Orleans, her festivals, rituals, and hospitality welcome you back every time. 'The Big Easy,' a term often invoked by tourists but seldom used by locals, is, in a way, a proper fit. Life was never easy here; yet, with its *laissez-faire* lifestyle, it is a city founded, and yes, grounded in easy pleasures.

A kudzu-covered path welcomes the foot traveler.

New Orleans' City Park gets a painterly portrait by photographer Josephine Sacabo.
Opposite: A bud begins to bloom in David Halliday's "Magnolia" series.

Once I saw a young man walking toward me on Dumaine Street, just as it crossed over into the lower end of Bourbon, a block from our house. He was of high-school age, olive-skinned, and was dressed in worn blue jeans and a plain white shirt. He would have gone unnoticed, except for the sunlight bouncing off an enormous second-hand brass tuba draped over his left shoulder and torso. With one hand, he was balancing the large instrument, and with the other, he was holding a fried chicken leg, which he was enjoying with gusto, gnawing it so that his head moved up and down with each bite. I'm not sure why, exactly, but the sight of it made me break into a grin. He may have been on his way to music class, or to some after-school rehearsal or to a play-for-tips gig as a street musician in a brass band just off Jackson Square. I'll never know, but I will always remember the sated, satisfied look on his face and his bouncing steps in his sneakers as he made his way through the French Quarter.

Life on Bourbon Street has been described as "the greatest free show on earth" by some, but it's true for all the city's other streets, too. The *Orléanais* live their lives in a constant embrace of *savoir vivré*, sitting on their front porches, leaning across patio fences, tipping their summer hats as they walk on the shady part of the sidewalk (still called banquettes by some) and marching in 'second lines' behind rag-tag street parades. For life here is never saved up, but is always, instead, savored.

Two gorgeous flowering magnolias capture the light.

THREE *The House Finds Us*

At heart, we were walkers who had fallen in love with a walking city.

Being city dwellers all our married lives, and New Yorkers for more than a decade, my husband and I were used to navigating our days – our lives, it seemed – on foot. And so we enjoyed the urban flavor of the shops and cafés that were scattered chock-a-block throughout New Orleans' *Vieux Carré*. After two centuries of existence, the founding French's name for the old quarter stuck, and a local might as easily say *"Vieux Carré,"* as "French Quarter," or simply "the Quarter" while dropping the "r" so it sounded like "Qwah-tah." These interchangeable phrases still ring through the air today, but there is no mistaking the speaker's intent – to convey the heart of what made New Orleans a European city in America, along with its own music, food, language and rituals. The Quarter, called "a living museum" by historians due to its well-preserved 17th and 18th Century cityscape of narrow streets and landmark houses, is a thriving, bustling neighborhood. Here, residents mix easily with tourists.

As frequent visitors, we always settled into one of the many antique-filled rooms of Soniat House, a tiny jewel box of a hotel on the prettiest and quietest residential stretch of Chartres Street. I adored its high-canopied beds, its *toile de Jouy*-covered walls, and its small, romantic European touches of fresh flowers, small paintings, woven tapestries and the old, uneven, hand-cut bricks of its courtyard walls. Each room's decor varied, and I had my favorites. I had memorized each suite's decor by room number so that whenever I phoned from New York to make reservations, I could rattle off my preferences to the desk clerk as he checked for availability.

Soniat's entry way, which had been an old *porte-cochere* or carriageway in the days when one arrived by equine, was framed by a beautiful wrought iron gate. Once inside its shady, bricked-in courtyard, I was charmed by its jumbo-sized palm fronds and tropical ferns, a gurgling

An American flag proudly flies in front of Soniat House hotel in the *Vieux Carré*.

fountain, gas-lit lanterns and bistro chairs scattered hospitably through-out. The sight of it had a Pavlovian effect on me. I immediately shifted from my harried travel mode to full-fledged holiday languor.

We enjoyed leisurely mornings sipping *café au lait* and nibbling the ho-tel's homemade biscuits, which were warmed by a heated brick wrapped in linen cloth and delivered in a small sweetgrass basket. Tucked inside was a small jar of homemade strawberry preserves made from the finest fruit of nearby Ponchatoula, Louisiana, the self-proclaimed 'Strawberry Capital of the World.' In the early evenings, we helped ourselves to flutes of Champagne, always imbibed in one of the hotel's two beautiful court-yards, before setting out for Galatoire's or Restaurant August or another of the city's famed dining spots. The New Orleans we had grown to love was waiting just outside our hotel door, and we departed each day with a sense of grand adventure. We usually walked downriver to the jazz clubs sprinkled along the 600 block of Faubourg Marigny's Frenchmen Street or upriver through the artsy Warehouse District on the Quarter's opposite side. We loved our Soniat routine, yet at a certain point, my latent nesting instincts began to override the conveniences connected to room or bar service.

The more time we spent in New Orleans, the more I began to dream of a house. During my long afternoon walks through the Quarter, I memorized its streets, studied its architecture, soaked in the pastel-colored cottages, each with their plantation shutters painted in contrast-ing colors. I gazed past tall wrought iron gates into the lush foliage of semi-hidden courtyards. I especially admired the old Colonial and Greek Revival houses. Their ornate balcony railings, called galleries, held large tumble-down bouquets of blooming bougainvillea and Confederate jasmine, all drenched in the radiant Southern light. I took note of every leafy magnolia tree, surveyed every patch of broken pavement, and even-tually, almost as if I had willed it to happen, a house found us.

In my mind, the house first appeared to us in the form of a prescient toast given by my husband. We were at a lovely party in the Garden District, thrown in our honor by a couple we had known for a dozen years. We were dining in a narrow hall lit by candlelight, sitting at a long table with twenty-four friends, all of whom we'd become close to in our years of visits. Looking back, I can no longer recall my husband's exact words – chatter and too much Champagne and the clatter of courses, all punctuated by a piano and jazz singer in the next room, by then had deafened any audible conversation. But my husband rose, gave thanks to our host and hostess, and said that he hoped we would one day put down

It takes a special kind of person to choose New Orleans over most of America... You have to be the kind who can dance at a funeral and spend thousands of dollars on plastic trinkets just for the privilege of throwing them off a tractor-driven float to complete strangers.

—Justin Lundgren

roots in what had become our beloved, adopted city. Glasses raised, his words applauded, we commenced our celebration. It was a Saturday night in early August. By ten o'clock the next morning, we would be standing in the side hall of our soon-to-be house on Dumaine Street.

The morning after our party, our late-night hostess placed an early wake-up call urging us to go look at a house five blocks away. "Hurry," she said, "the listing won't last." So we scrambled out the door, and sized up the house through a restaurant window across the street. In the time it took to down a hasty breakfast of *café au lait* and *beignets*, we summoned the realtor and secured the keys that led us inside. The exterior was classic but simple: gray stucco, dark green shutters, a full gallery hanging overhead, all of which we would soon discover obscured the large, charming interior just inside its front door.

Contrary to popular wisdom, real estate is *not* all about location. For me, it's a trinity: one-part construction, one-part location, and the last part, emotion. When all are in sync, a house has claimed you. It can either be a 'put-down-your-roots' home, or a way station through which you pass on your way to somewhere else. We knew at once that the house on Dumaine was the former. Besides, I must have dreamt of it. The moment we walked in, looked upwards at its high ceilings, then down the hallway to its small, leafy courtyard, it was familiar to me. Its walls, its winding stairway seemed like a known and comfortable haven: a reflection of my mind's eye. The French term, *coup de foudre*, or love at first sight, said it best. Where another person might have seen right angles or a marbled fireplace, I saw the clear backdrop for our lives in New Orleans.

A sense of place is not where you live; it's where you feel. Your body can be in one place but your heart can be in another.

— James Carville

Palms pervade the portico, patio and *port cochère* of Soniat House.

Though the 1850's house had been expertly renovated by its owner-architect just a few years earlier, now it wore a tired coat of once-white paint that had aged into a creamy patina. I could feel the absence of color, and thought to myself, a house with colorful rooms might lead to a colorful life. By then, my eyes were resting on imaginary silks and linens and seeing patterns at play, and rooms lit by chandeliers, with happy people clinking glasses, surrounded by food and laughter and music. We would fill up these rooms, and a townhouse would be perfect for us. One hardly ever outgrows a townhouse; one simply settles in.

We sealed the deal that same day over Sazeracs, the city's official cocktail, at the historic Napoleon House before boarding our flight home. Then, just three weeks later, before we were scheduled to sign the sale papers, Hurricane Katrina's force broke the city's levees, which flooded New Orleans, and created the largest man-made disaster in United States history. Thousands of its residents were left homeless, or lost, or worse, as the world watched and debated the viability of 'America's Venice,' a city below sea level, and its chances for survival. Did we really still want to own a dream house in a city that was eighty percent underwater?

It's certainly a defiant little place,
like a secret soul for the rest of the country.

—Dave Matthews

Back in New York, our hearts broke as friends weighed in to comfort us in that somber, down-turn way that disaster evokes and advised us to forego the bid on the house. "Step away," they said. Even as we soul-searched our options, my husband, a writer, was asked to pen a column in *Town & Country* magazine. The article was called "New Orleans on My Mind," and in it, he reminisced about the good times we'd had in the city that had been a frequent stage not only for our married life, but also for our courtship and early romance. My husband added that rueful refrain that "the gods laugh at those who plan."

The author's *garçonniére*, melding French and African design, is nicknamed 'the swamp' due to its algae-inspired hues of pink and green.

Straw & Silk

Behind the three stories of our house on Dumaine, lies an addition, called a *garçonniére*. I first thought this to be some vestige of slave housing, but instead discovered that it was a small bachelor apartment, which, in the French Creole fashion, housed the dweller's oldest son. The *garçonniére* is its own respite, its own oasis. It is a room with no purpose, just a fantasy sitting room, an absolute extravagance for people like us who had been closely confined to condominium living for decades.

The *garçonniére* is bordered on one side by two sets of French doors. When opened, they bring the visitor eye-level with a flowering banana tree, a ready-made umbrella accented with blooming purple buds. It overlooks the courtyard and offers an indoor-outdoor space where guests can sit, sip a cocktail, take in the garden, nap or read through the afternoon. A group might gather for a late, rainy supper high above the courtyard. In summer, we open the French doors during daily rainstorms just to hear the drops of water splash against the brick courtyard and the slate roof overhead.

Fortunately, it *was* too late for us. We had already been swept away, many years before. Souls searched. City mourned. The worst imagined. And then, miraculously, we made a decision rooted less in reason and more in just plain hope: we decided to stay the course. We bought the house three months later, in November 2005, as soon as the city's courthouse re-opened. In fact, we were one of the first home purchases in the *Vieux Carré*, post-Katrina, and were on our way to becoming a part of what would be the *new* New Orleans.

New Orleans seemed at times like a dream in the imagination of her striving populace, a dream held intact at every second by a tenacious, though unconscious, collective will.

—Anne Rice

The Tale of the Tassels

Well before the idea of a New Orleans house cast its spell over me, on a weekend trip to Paris, I spotted a bin of silk tassels in a tiny hardware store sequestered in one of the winding, hidden streets within the 6th *arrondissement*. The colors were a luscious mixed bouquet of soft pastels and bold hues: peony shades of white and pink, a cornflower blue, an icy aqua, a hot 'Schiaparelli' pink, a wasabi green and a bright fuchsia. I bought them as Parisian souvenirs but they had unknowingly become talismans. In the end, I couldn't bear to part with them. Eventually, I carried them to New Orleans and tucked them inside an old Limoges terrine I had rescued from the back room of a Magazine Street antiques shop, along with a dozen oyster plates in the same pattern. One day, I opened the lid and said to myself, "These are the colors for the house."

Meanwhile, on the heels of the storm, as a new homeowner without a list of contractors, painters, upholsterers or service workers, and knowing that even if I had that list, workers were in short supply given the needs of our devastated, flooded city. I was blindingly resolute. After eight months of missed appointments, no-shows, and unanswered calls to my pleas for renovation help, Hal Williamson entered our lives.

An antique tassel matches the patina of a Provincial armoire.

Dual Reflections in Double Parlors

The house is Greek Revival. Its overriding characteristics are symmetry and balance. Here, pairs prevail in double parlors with twin fireplaces and matching Italian chandeliers. Columns, mantles and pocket doors are arranged in the most companionable duos. Pairs of silver candlesticks top connecting demilunes. Twin terra cotta angels stand sentry on the front mantle. A pair of wooden turtle doves perch within the carved woodwork of a French Provincial armoire. Adjoining parlors, both upstairs and downstairs, are painted in tone-on-tone pink and purple, and blue and green, in Creole colors chosen from historical paint chips. Bourbon Street Blue mixes with Bienville Green. Creole Pink borders a Dauphine Street Beige.

After decades of living in small, urban apartment buildings, we decided that any upstairs room beyond our master bedroom, and the obligatory living and dining rooms, would be 'not a bedroom.' Each of these 'extra' rooms would have a defined purpose, mostly focused on the recurring themes of our favorite pastimes: puttering, napping and reading while listening for hours to the strains of my husband's jazz collection. There would be a library for books, a sitting room for reading and watching old movies, and my ultimate fantasy, a connecting parlor or *boudoir* just off the main bedroom. Not a single room would be taken up with large, domineering beds, waiting empty for guests between visits. The truth is that we enjoy playing hosts for long, lively dinner parties, spontaneous luncheons and endless cocktail hours, but we are not good at breakfasts.

Sumptuous silk offers inspiration for the interior's palette. *Opposite:* The front parlor is arranged tone-on-tone in pink and purple.

Pairs of objects appear throughout the double parlors.

Hal owned an antiques shop on Chartres Street. I stopped by one day and we struck up a friendly conversation. As Southerners often do, we squared off and began listing family trees and places of birth until we settled on a commonality: we soon discovered we were linked by Alabama roots on both sides. We were as good as cousins, with similar backgrounds and close in age. I asked Hal, on the spot, to leave his shop and walk the four blocks to our empty, unpainted, unfurnished house. Being his agreeable self, he followed me obligingly, and once inside our front door, I attempted a hasty introduction between him and my unsuspecting husband, blurting out the words, "This is Hal. He's our new decorator."

Within minutes, I had shown Hal the tassels; he took one look and nodded, and smiled. "I've got it," he said, returning them to the terrine. Fortunately, Hal has a knack for memorizing colors. Weeks later, he showed up with a dramatically embroidered silk fabric with the exact hues of the tassels' lavender, purple, blue and aqua, set against a bed of cream. We backed it with a bright turquoise gingham. From it, Hal created a duvet and matching pillows for our bedroom. On the day the wondrous bedding arrived, my husband and our dogs, Louis and Ella, lay down on top of it. Man and beasts fell into a two-hour nap.

Paper, Paint & Passamenterie

Neither Hal nor I were New Orleans natives, but our sense of kinship and shared love of the city grew deeper with each project we tackled as we worked to transform the house into a home.

I wanted glorious color-upon-color on every floor, like the stacked jewel tones of Ladurèe confection boxes in Paris' most famous *pâtisserie*. I craved colors that recalled objects: the blue-green of a robin's egg, or the custom-blended blue-teal of a Tiffany box, all grounded by stained coffee-colored floors. Once painted, the downstairs parlors paired an eggplant purple with a carnation pink. To this, we added shining pieces of mixed metal tones: bits of mercury glass, sterling silver pieces and iridescent silks. Double chandeliers were hung in both parlors and twinkled and winked at their reflections in the large silver-plated mirrors hung above original onyx mantles. Our friend, author and photographer Susan Sully, called this the "gun metal and roses" approach.

We conceived the house as a colorful play of light and shadow, with pastel rooms punctuated by contrasting shades of silk and linen. We juxtaposed dramatically different textures, like silk next to straw, and dupioni

Feminine touches echo from desktop to dressing table.

next to coarse linen. In the front parlor, Hal and I placed a French settee upholstered in rough plum linen next to the shimmering velvet of two high-backed, winged Louis XV chairs upholstered in a plush taupey-gray, which prompted an editor friend to christen them "the Weimaraners."

I became single-minded in my pursuit of furnishings. Within weeks, I had found Napoleon III chairs, a hand-carved Swedish Gustavian bench, Louis XV *bergeres*, and Louis XVI *fauteuils* – twenty-three chairs in all. My husband urged me to purchase mundane items such as beds and perhaps a dining room table. Instead, without breaking stride, I moved on to china and porcelain.

Femme, Femme, Femme

The house is feminine. There are little surprises of miniature tiaras and crowns throughout, a New Orleans reference to both its royal French founders and its bevy of Carnival queens. Gold crowns are pinned to a sequined evening bag, along with tiny gilded *fleur-de-lys*. As a surprise from Hal, a pair of regal crowns were white-stitched into the powder blue silk valances atop our bedroom curtains. Beneath them, an exaggerated cipher spells out our collective initials, *D, J* and *S*. Crowns appear on stationery and linens. Smaller replicas made of wire, or of paste and paper hide between books on bookshelves and reign from the tops of desk corners.

Purple velvet and gilt dress up a French *bergère*. *Opposite:* Petite gardenias gathered from the courtyard rest on a nightstand.

"*Guillotine*" windows provide panels of light amid the blue-drenched master bedroom. *Opposite:* The "altar" to jazz great Ella Fitzgerald is draped with pink "ballroom" curtains and a matching marble-topped desk.

Muses, captured by both camera and paintbrush, watch silently from nearly every room. Downstairs, a French oil painting of a young Creole girl gazes at us from pale pink living room walls. A shy nude, eyes looking downward and in a sly stance with her hands clasped in front of her, stands full-length next to the front parlor fireplace across from her more coiffed, costumed companion. Both are creations of French painter, Patrick Pietropoli. A young child raises her hands in mid-air in a photographic 'Christ pose,' while a palmetto-laden belle hides amid a swampy terrain in a watery portrait on cool blue walls.

A more recognizable duo of queens – one of gospel and one of jazz – hold a prominent place in our house: the presence of musical artists Ella Fitzgerald and New Orleans native Mahalia Jackson reside here. The latter is immortalized in a large, dramatic silkscreen by New Orleans artist Richard Thomas. Her skin is painted a royal purple, her eyes are open wide and her mouth is alive with song. The lights from the chandelier above provide Queen Mahalia with a most-righteous gospel crown, while shining a splendorous spotlight upon her.

The second-floor landing plays host to what we lovingly call 'the Ella altar' – a resplendent black-and-white portrait of the Jazz empress that was taken during her performance at the New Orleans Jazz & Heritage Festival's tenth anniversary celebration. She is clearly enjoying the moment, smiling broadly in a full-length silk taffeta evening gown, and glancing at admirers who watch in the wings. The photo stands above the most ornate piece in the townhouse, a carved, French *Rococo* desk topped with pink marble. Fittingly, it is here that we stage the local jazz students from the New Orleans Center for Creative Arts (NOCCA) at cocktail parties and candlelight suppers. Unseen, they play from above. Guests hear the music and assume the sound is reverberating from some state-of-the-art audio system. But, these are real, fledgling jazz artists. They play and improvise away on a tiny landing, a make-shift stage in front of Ella and her floor-length 'ball gown' silk curtains in a dusty pink, to coordinate with the matching walls and to pay homage to her in her party dress.

Purple walls are offset by purple *toile* and a silkscreen portrait of New Orleans-born gospel singer Mahalia Jackson.

Rod Cook's *"Swamp Belle"* portrait hangs in the upstairs parlor. *Opposite:* A scene of siblings re-enacting a "Christ pose" by Raymond Meeks hangs in the foyer.

French dining chairs upholstered in custom *toile* illustrate scenes from the city's history.

Grandmother's Gardenias

My favorite nook in the house is our small bricked-in courtyard. It is bordered by a series of French doors on one side, and a high, hand-cut brick wall on the other. Here, I indulge in what is perhaps my recurring Proust 'madeleine' moment: just sitting and inhaling the fragrance of my late grandmother's petite gardenias. My Aunt Ruth brought them from her Florida garden with their roots floating in tiny jars of water, having already uprooted them once from their Alabama birthplace, her own mother's garden, stem-by-stem. These transplanted gardenias are to me the fanciest and the whitest of flowers, and give off the sweet long-ago scent of my grandmother's perfume. She adored gardenias, both in her garden and her *toilette*. The flowers bloom like miniature *boutonnières* atop the leafy green foliage. On late spring mornings, I often sit near them, as if in my own little world as I read the day's newspapers, still in my nightgown. The cold brick floor, beaded from the wet morning dew, cools my bare feet. I breathe slowly, and listen, not to the quiet, but to my own choir of noises: the cooing sighs of morning doves who perch like statuary on the tops of my courtyard wall. They are joined by a cacophony of crickets, steamboat whistles, children playing in the Catholic school playground across the street, cathedral bells, the clop of horse hooves from the passing sight-seeing carriages, and a duo of voices, one male and the other female. For each day, the 'Pie Lady' sings out the fresh flavors of her homemade fruit pies *a cappella* as she pushes her small pie buggy through Quarter streets. 'Mr. Okra' cruises slowly about the neighborhood in his farmer's truck, reciting his bass-like, sing-song melody: "I have ok-ra . . . I have to-ma-toes . . . I have wa-ter-me-lon." As if performing a spontaneous duet, their voices rise above both sidewalk and street, and mingle mid-air into one sweet, tuneful aria.

All these sounds are comforting to me as I sit in my tiny, inner courtyard divided by half-shade and half-sun. There I have planted a mix of sago palms accented by my grandmother's white gardenias, and an occasional pink bromeliad. Each time we leave town for any period of time, the untended garden turns to jungle. The palmetto leaves grow so big that the sun's rising and setting projects large shadows on the side of the house. The leaves are heavy, and dance and wave in wind and rain, yet they always survive any storm or squall that passes over our home, much like New Orleans, herself.

A magnolia floats in a Limoges bowl set upon a *toile*-covered chair.

The palm fronds of our jumbo-sized banana trees hang low, the umbrella effect heightened by the sheer weight of its ripe, budding clusters. They bounce and wink at their faux image just beyond the French doors inside the kitchen. Beyond the landing, a Martinique banana tree wallpaper made famous by the Beverly Hills Hotel offsets peach-colored terra cotta floors.

Now that we have settled in, the house on Dumaine Street is like a character in our lives. After years of living in small urban spaces, we finally have a real house, big enough to gather all our friends. The dining room table, a much-beloved antique, is sturdy enough to hold a suckling pig. The house never disappoints, and always upholds its end of the bargain. It welcomes and expands to meet the hordes of family and friends who come together on holidays and found weekends, and sometimes made-up occasions.

On the eve of a milestone birthday, we gathered friends from East Coast, Gulf Coast, from New York and New Orleans (and Paris and other parts, too) to celebrate – not just the occasion at hand – but also the house and the city. That was my birthday wish. We hired a brass band and threw ourselves a joyous housewarming. We chose a menu of favorite local dishes: shrimp and biscuits, crabmeat, grits and grillades, and pralines. Music played into the night, and with the help of too much Champagne, our guests lost track of time.

The house continues to pull us in, and soothe us. Once inside, we are rewarded by peace and quiet, which is, to me, one thing that no amount of planning, charm, money or work can get you when you're in New York City. This is no longer the 'faraway place' we travel to; it has become the 'familiar.' Here, inside its cool walls and brick-bordered courtyard garden, the house anchors my husband and me, but it also surprises us.

One afternoon, during our first spring there, I forgot to close the French doors at the end of the front hall leading to our courtyard. It was late April and a rainstorm lingered overhead. I turned the key to enter and was overtaken by the mixture of light and scent permeating the hallway from the garden. As twilight faded and night descended, a lone gas lantern flickered in the dusk, amid shadows of swaying banana leaves. Traces of wet soil and damp, moss-covered brick mingled with gardenia, and sweet olive to fill the downstairs rooms. It was as though I had entered into my own secret garden. I stepped inside and closed the door behind me. I was home.

Bouquets of gardenias appear in every room of the townhouse.

FOUR *Monograms & Muslin*

The Monogram as Metaphor

Once inside the hushed, formal foyers of New Orleans' grand, historic houses, curious interlopers have only to glance in a single direction to encounter a curlicue of letters, intertwined in a marriage of design or cipher, or a solitary initial signifying a surname. The item that bears it – be it valance, pillow, mantle, garden gate or ceiling – has been lovingly stamped with New Orleanians' traditional, much loved declaration of ownership: the monogram.

Below the Mason-Dixon line, the monogram is a metaphor. As a whole, Southerners take special pride in their lineage and are proud of its far-reaching past. For many, monograms have endured as a classic, timeless element of design. Like the crown motif, which has both embossed and embroidered its way across the city, the monogram, an early mark of a sovereign's signature, is yet another reference to New Orleans' royal past. Initials are stitched onto table linens, letter-pressed upon the corners of correspondence, and woven through the lives of families for generations. Lacking a family crest, one can always monogram.

In the center of Jackson Square, the very heart of the *Vieux Carré*, I stand eye-level with the city's most famous initials: recurring cast-iron ribbons of second- and third-story balcony railings that bear, in cursive letters, the characters 'A' and 'P.' They symbolize two legendary New Orleans surnames, Almonester and Pontalba. There, along the rows of red Louisiana brick townhouses, these ciphers honor both the maiden and married names of Baroness Micaela Pontalba, a native daughter who returned from Paris after a disastrous marriage to a French cousin. Once home, she developed two symmetrical plots of inherited, prime real estate flanking Jackson Square in the old city's center. Inspired by the *Palais Royal* and the *Place des Vosges* in Paris, the Baroness commissioned the span of lacy ironwork in 1849 to embrace her lasting civic contribution:

Antique embroidered French linens spell out the first initials of their owners.

An array of monograms are stitched on hand towels from Leontine Linens.

the largest apartments ever erected in the city. Today, they are recognized as historical landmarks and, although leased by city and state, keys to these *exquis appartements* are now passed down through generations. Greek architectural references and Creole breezeways leading up to long, curving staircases, Parisian flourishes and a mansard roof attract tourists from around the globe, who gather to photograph the Baroness' buildings and to trace her monogram within the iron script.

Ciphers & Carnival Crowns

In the tradition of the Baroness Pontalba's bequest to the city, two notable present day New Orleanians are leaving their mark here by creating heirloom quality items that are among the city's best exports (next to jazz and *beignet* mix, of course!)

New Orleanians are event-motivated. They arrange their lives around the plentiful, important social gatherings for both Carnival and café society. They live to be entertained and to entertain.

—Rosemary James

New Orleans native Alexa Pulitzer's bespoke stationery has an Old World quality. As the proprietor of Alexa Pulitzer, LLC, she often prints finely-milled, monogrammed Italian papers, sold under her brand, Alexa Pulitzer, in her favorite colors of aubergine, slate blue, olive, copper and espresso. As a young student in Italy, she found inspiration in the Renaissance period. Alexa employs antique Roman styles for men and fanciful Victorian or Baroque styles for women, and she is known for making clever use of ciphers. She was the first stationer to turn the Carnival theme on its head with her playful calling cards and invitations bearing crowns and tiaras with distinctive imprints ranging from a classic *fleur-de-lis* to a swampy Louisiana alligator king in full coronation regalia. Alexa is so committed to the city of her birth that she has virtually branded it through the icons featured in her whimsical designs. Beyond Carnival season, customers can embrace their inner royalty, or opt for stationery bearing her iconic New Orleans emblems of French *bergeres*, chandeliers, jazz trumpets and palmetto fronds.

Alexa Pulitzer's fanciful designs incorporate French crowns and *fleur-de-lys*.

A purse pinned with crowns and *fleur-de-lys* tops a stack of hand-lettered stationery.
Opposite: A trio of letters create a feminine monogram for the owner of Leontine Linens.

Monograms & Muslin

As a young bride-to-be, Jane Scott Hodges discovered her grandmother's wedding *trousseau* in her parents' attic in Kentucky and grew so enamored with these fine monogrammed linens that she later founded Leontine Linens, named after the New Orleans street where she lived.

According to Jane Scott, today's New Orleanian has her (or his) grandmother's sensibilities but is bolder when it comes to choosing heirloom-quality linens. While previous generations limited their linen colors to white and ecru, today's collector finds that ivory is a better 'mixer' and goes with everything. (This being New Orleans, where old customs are classics, white-on-white is still popular.) Jane Scott was once quoted in a magazine as saying that if you choose an ivory linen and add a gold thread for the monogram, you've created the 'little black dress' version of the table napkin. (In New Orleans, gold, like gilt, is a neutral that easily mixes with silver, whether on the table, as jewelry, or at the annual Mardi Gras encounter of Rex and Comus – see Chapter One).

There is a culture here that is very precious, beautiful, and unduplicated.

—Tom Piazza

Today's linen collector, unlike past generations, embraces the motto 'bigger is better.' The French influence is seen in her oversized 'lapkin,' or large napkin measuring 24 by 24 inches. And, today's monogram is also larger, as well as being more the focus of an item, and not the linen itself. Jane Scott advises her customers to find inspiration from the past, such as re-creating your initials in the same style as your grandmother's, but to add your own color combination and use your linen with new things that you've collected. The layered look of old with new, like gold with silver, is a New Orleans hallmark in decorating and entertaining. Jane Scott quotes her mentor, New Orleans' designer Melissa Rufty, who famously said, "A room should never look as if everything arrived on the same day."

Jane Scott Hodges' Tips for Monogramming:

1 A monogram should always reflect your personal style. Don't be intimidated by the rules of a bygone era. Your monogram is a personal expression and should be as customized as your home.

2 By all means, use different styles of lettering in different venues. Not every monogram should be identical. Some ideas: incorporate your spouse's letters into the linens for the master bed or bath; recreate your grandmother's napkins in your own letters; or use a single surname initial for the guest room towels.

3 Invest in and use special items to enhance the memories of enjoying them and give them extra importance. Pull your linens out of the closet and put them to good – no, great – use!

4 Don't be afraid of color. White-on-white is classic and timeless but peach with indigo would look wonderful with your Imari china!

5 Don't focus on thread-count (though Jane Scott's preference is the 500-count). She suggests Italian-milled Egyptian cotton for quality and livability.

FIVE *Recipes & Rituals*

In New Orleans, all food is infused with ritual. The past is repast. Weeks invariably begin with Monday's 'wash day' menu of red beans and rice, and end with long, languid (and yes, liquid!) lunches at Galatoire's, or another white-linen establishment. Restaurant fare features all kinds of shellfish (oysters, crab, crawfish, shrimp) and seafood galore (flounder, snapper, catfish, pompano). The Vatican may have repealed the fish-only Fridays rule, but in a city of tradition, the large Catholic clientele hasn't changed its ways. You begin the week here with red beans and end it with red snapper. Both rituals hold true today, whether you're Catholic or Episcopalian, a bona-fide Mayflower descendant or a transplanted New Yorker.

All seasons, particularly the social ones, are celebrated with great tradition. The months between Thanksgiving and Memorial Day are jammed with jazz and literary *fêtes*, debutante balls, art walks, opera and ballet season, museum and gallery openings. There are a whole host of holidays not celebrated in the 'other' America: *Réveillon* dinners, countless parades and masked balls, Twelfth Night, and, of course, Carnival ending with Mardi Gras. While every meal here, both high and low, is its own occasion, my favorite gatherings are the small, informal progressive suppers thrown with our neighbors in the French Quarter, where walking from house-to-townhouse-to-cottage is often a three- or four-course affair. Each neighbor is impresario, chef and bartender when the entourage stops for a bite and a cocktail *chez* host.

As a Southerner, I know true hospitality when I see it, yet the *Orléanais* are the consummate convivial creatures. In a city known for forty food festivals a year, an exhaustive list of world-class restaurants and too many star chefs to count, Southern hospitality combines French table service, European flavors and Creole traditions. The result: a population of charming, outgoing, epicureans. Locals dine out so frequently that, in older establishments like Antoine's and Galatoire's, regular customers have both a house account and a personal waiter. In fact, New Orleans author Peter Feibleman wrote that when he was a child, an uncle warned

Oysters bathed in *mignonette* are served up in antique Limoges as a savory first course.

him, "You can't let an unknown waiter serve you," explaining that it was "akin to eating on the floor." I understand; I have friends who will not darken a restaurant's doorway unless hand-chipped ice chills their cocktails, and the sugar bowl is as pure and un-adulterated as the driven snow, meaning, pre-packaged packets are *n'est pas fait!* Both food and service matter equally. Dining is an experience, an occasion to be savored and *never* just a meal.

Menu & Memory

I, myself, am a great 'trader' of recipes. For me, a recipe is more than the sum of ingredients on a list; each is a written history, a culinary legacy of a region that is in touch with, and constantly harks back to, its ancestry. "New Orleans cooks," Feibleman wrote, "tend to have personal kitchen quirks that don't always go into (written) recipes." For this reason, nearly every master (and mistress) of the kitchen will offer copious verbal instructions on how a dish is prepared, where to find the best ingredients, how to serve it and what to serve it with. Here, menu begets memory; taste becomes testimonial. What you eat informs who you are.

Among all gatherings of Southerners, the favorite topic during any meal will be the meal at hand. New Orleanians joke that when supper begins, the discussion starts with "What's for dessert?" Meal time is also the occasion to exchange new restaurant recommendations, what old haunts to revisit, which recipes to retrieve from the files for the next party, what's in season, what's in your garden, who your favorite suppliers are, how a dish was prepared – ingredient-by-ingredient – and where the recipe originated. The standard answer to, "May I ask for the recipe," elicits the automatic, "Yes, you may have it." Is there another American enclave where every local citizen is a foodie? You could actually walk into the cool night with a new favorite recipe in your hand from every home you visit here. People do.

Cocktails & Conversation

I have my own list of what makes entertaining in the Crescent City so special. There are few food rules here where food rules. Here are a few observations:

In New Orleans, carbohydrates are never a sin: bread will be broken, be it hand-beaten biscuits, freshly-baked French *boules* or grandmother's cornbread recipe.

Champagne chills in an antique silver bucket during the cocktail hour.

Charmed, Seduced & Sated

My friend Alexa wouldn't dream of *not* monogramming the cocktail napkins and always gathers trumpet flowers and palm fronds from her backyard to decorate the table. "I always open the doors and windows to bring the fragrant smells from my garden inside," she says. "Who needs candles when you have jasmine and gardenias outside?" In typical New Orleans fashion, hosts share their recipes *and* their gardens. Cut flowers from garden or patio are carried inside, a favorite jar of home-grown figs will be pressed into your hands as you depart into the night. Rich soil, afternoon rain in spring and summer and an almost year-round tropical climate guarantee roses, camellias, gardenias, magnolias, jasmine, palmettos, decorative ferns and all kinds of fruits, vegetables and herbs to even the most fickle home gardeners.

Cherry "cokes" and Ponchatoula strawberries are beloved regional favorites.

Both rustic and formal elements of a meal will be combined in a way that sometimes takes my breath away. Simple dishes will be opulently served: seafood gumbo in a Limoges terrine; mother's fig preserves in grandmother's cut-crystal dish, topped with homemade ice cream scooped from a porcelain *'rafraichissoir â verres.'*

Prized possessions from the past – wedding china, heirloom linens, the family silver service and any unique serving piece to be found in cupboard and attic – will be used in everyday ways. Crawfish may be served in a crystal fingerbowl, or deviled eggs arranged on antique oyster plates.

Experienced hosts often have complete, monogrammed sets of French-sized napkins (always cloth, never paper!) and oyster forks (sterling, not silver-plate!) that match the deviled-egg forks and long, elegant iced tea spoons. No host here is intimidated by formality; treasures are to be used, shared, and enjoyed at every opportunity. So, for instance, china and crystal will be packed up for picnics, and even plastic 'go' cups will be emblazoned with the hosts' Carnival krewe insignia.

Even the busiest hosts will make sure the *canapés* are homemade. And, as guests, we'll likely sit down to a delicious meal in which a tried-and-true heirloom recipe, or several, has found its way into a course of two. The food will invariably be prepared from fresh local ingredients. (Long before the idea of a locavore, New Orleanians celebrated down-home delicacies such as Creole tomatoes, Ponchatoula strawberries, and a year-round supply of Louisiana oysters, Gulf shrimp, crabmeat, crawfish and other seafood.)

Bartenders, waiters and musicians make regular appearances at large and small gatherings. These trained professionals proudly help uphold the city's standards for entertaining.

Be prepared to plunge into an authentic cocktail hour. At every party, a full bar service, fully bartendered or self-serve, is always set up within easy reach of guests. Cocktails, having been created here, are such a part of New Orleans culture, that we know we'll be served the real thing: a Sazerac, an Old-Fashioned, a Sidecar or perhaps an orange-scented Ramos Gin Fizz. And, the French tradition of Champagne and Champagne *apéritifs* is alive and well. The list of libations will have a retro, yet grown-up spin – no sweet blender drinks, nor trendy cocktails with trendy names created just for the occasion. Drink in hand, the hosts will make proper introductions, followed by lively conversation, none of which will ask – or care – "What do you do?" The first question is always, "What do you drink?"

Entertaining in New Orleans is all about the distinguished architecture, sultry weather, divine food, cultural diversity, joie de vivre and the generous expressive people of New Orleans.

— Alexa Pulitzer

And, unless temperance is involved, count on alcohol to close the meal as a perfect bookend to the opening cocktail hour. Even the sweets here support this concept: I can always spot a Southern dessert due to the whisky sauce, rum-soaked raisins, *crème de menthe* topping or whipped, alcohol-laden 'hard' sauce.

I never cease to marvel at how hosts in The Big Easy make it all look so easy. One hostess I know planned and cooked the entire menu for her daughter's very 'uptown' wedding of 300 without batting an eyelash. Another well-known party giver took cocktails in her courtyard, alone, every day for a week leading up to a garden party to rehearse the sunset as her guests would experience it. She watched the sun fade and disappear then lined up her patio chairs to avoid direct sunlight and to face the setting sun.

Champagne cocktails feature kumquats preserved in Cointreau liqueur.

"My only regret is that I did
not drink more Champagne."
Lord Maynard Keynes
(on his deathbed)

"My only regret is that I did not drink more Champagne."

Lord Maynard Keynes
(on his deathbed)

Ode to an Oyster, Serenade to a Shrimp

My great affection for Southern food is based partially on the love of the familiar – delicious tastes from an Alabama childhood. I was raised on an abundance of shellfish from the Gulf of Mexico and farm-fresh produce straight from the garden. So, whenever I compose a menu, I hark back, always, to a single favorite ingredient: the oyster, the crab or another shellfish, the pecan or the egg. Most of the recipes that follow are based on one of these three items, and many were happily provided by friends who have prepared these very dishes for my husband and me. So, please, pull up a chair, raise a glass, and prepare to taste my city's flavors.

Drinking Kumquats at Christmas

When Hal Williamson moved from a French Quarter townhouse to a grand historic home in the Garden District, he inherited a mini-orchard of kumquat trees. Kumquats are plentiful in Louisiana, and small and delicate enough to use in decorations or as a garnish. (Hal's Christmas wreathes feature magnolia leaves dotted with kumquat clusters and he fills Old Paris urns with pineapples and then uses kumquats to decorate their lips.) Kumquats were a popular fruit with the early Creole people of New Orleans, and armed with kumquats' heritage, their luscious orange color and tart taste, and the abundance in his own backyard, Hal began to cook with them. (No orchard handy? Kumquats can also be grown in containers or courtyards.)

Here are two of Hal's favorite recipes: tasty kumquat marmalade for breakfast brioche or an afternoon serving of *pâté*; and Creole Kumquat Champagne Cocktails. A holiday batch of the marmalade will keep till summer, when it can be used as a cool and refreshing treat. Parisian versions of the Champagne Cocktail are accented with the flavors of currants or peaches, so why not kumquats? Lovely to see, sip and eat, and delicious when served with traditional sides such as roasted, salted pecans and cheese straws.

HAL'S CREOLE KUMQUAT CHAMPAGNE COCKTAIL

INGREDIENTS:

1 cup of kumquats
(smallest variety, seeded)
½ cup of sugar
1 cup of Cointreau
(or orange-flavored liquor)

Slice each kumquat in half and remove the seeds with the tip of your knife (if using a larger kumquat variety, slice into smaller pieces). Place the fruit in a sauce pan, pour the sugar over them and turn the burner to medium-high. Pour the Cointreau over this mixture and stir just until the sugar is dissolved. Remove pan from the stove top and let cool to room temperature. After cooling, strain off the liquor to remove any seeds or bits. Spoon the fruits carefully back into their liquor and then store mixture in a decorative jar in the kitchen or bar area under refrigeration. Hal prefers a crystal biscuit jar.

To make the cocktail, spoon one of the kumquat halves or several small pieces into the bottom of a Champagne flute glass with a little bit of the liquor (about ½ teaspoon). Top with your favorite Champagne – chilled, of course.

HAL'S CREOLE KUMQUAT MARMALADE: *VOULEZ-VOUS MANGER AVEC MOI, CE SOIR?*

INGREDIENTS:

4 cups prepared kumquats
2½ cups water
⅛ tsp baking soda
1 box of fruit pectin
(Such as Sure-Jell)
½ tsp butter
5½ cups sugar, measured
into separate bowl

First thing: Wash jars and screw-bands in hot soapy water; rinse with warm water. Pour boiling water over flat lids in saucepan off the heat. Let stand in hot water until ready to use. Drain jars well before filling.

Rinse and prepare to cut 4 cups of kumquats by cutting them into about 6 pieces per fruit, removing seeds as you go. Bring 2½ cups of water to boil. Add the fruit and any juice. Reduce heat to medium-low; cover and simmer for 20 minutes stirring occasionally. Cover and simmer an additional 10 minutes. Measure exactly 4 cups of this prepared fruit into a 6- or 8-qt. saucepot.

Stir one box of pectin into prepared fruit in saucepot. Add butter to reduce the foaming. Bring mixture to full boil on high heat, stirring constantly: this mixture should just not stop bubbling. Stir in sugar. Return to full robust boil and boil exactly 1 minute, stirring constantly. Remove from heat. Skim off any foam on the top.

Immediately ladle into prepared jars, filling to within ⅛ inch of tops. Wipe down jar rims and threads with a clean cloth. Cover with the two-piece lids and screw the bands tightly shut. Lower the jars into a large pot. Add boiling water and cover the jars by 1 to 2 inches over their tops. Cover this and bring the water to gentle boil for 10 minutes. Remove jars and place upright on towel to cool completely. After jars cool, check seals by pressing middles of lids with four fingers. If lids spring back, lids are not sealed and refrigeration is necessary.

Putting the "Ahhhh" in Pralines

Pralines, (pronounced prah-leens, not the touristy pray-leen!) are French Creole creations and classic, practically ubiquitous, New Orleans treats. They are the happy result of an abundance of pecans and sugar, the two main ingredients, and were named for the French Maréchal du Plessis-Praslin, Duke of Choiseul-Praslin, whose recipe led to the divine pralines of New Orleans. They are the city's version of the cookie and are sold fresh throughout the *Vieux Carré*, where they are baked in large ovens and wrapped in wax paper and sold by the piece. My husband and I like to serve them with the dessert course at dinner parties, hot from the kitchen. They are their most delicious when fresh and warm, and especially when passed on silver trays with a *demitasse* of bitter, rich chicory coffee.

While New Orleanians have high expectations when it comes to taste, aroma and seasoning, they are anything but snobs in their appreciation of a simple, unfussy recipe. In fact, my favorite praline recipe among dozens comes from a fifth-generation New Orleanian who clipped it years ago from the back of an electric bill. The crumbling original, copied many times over, was sent via mail in the days when mail was 'the mail' and not e-mail, snail mail or voice mail. Decades ago, monthly billing statements throughout the South included recipes and home economics tips. My source swears by it, saying "You really can't tell the difference and it's so quick and easy." He is right. My friend uses the pralines days later to crumble on top of vanilla ice cream as a wonderful dessert.

NEW ORLEANS STYLE MICROWAVE PRALINES

Combine brown sugar, corn syrup and whipping cream in an 8-cup microwave-safe bowl. Microwave on high 13 minutes, stirring every 2 minutes (or you may remove whipped cream mixture to test temperature, which should be between 234 and 240 degrees). Add butter and stir until mixture is well blended and begins to cool and get creamy. Stir in nuts and quickly drop by tablespoonfuls onto waxed paper to cool. (Note: if you lay newspaper underneath the waxed paper it will keep your counter neat.) These are always best when made on a day with lower humidity. Carefully remove pralines from paper and store between waxed paper layers in an airtight container.

Yields 30 pralines.

INGREDIENTS:

1 pound light brown sugar
2 tbsp light corn syrup
1 cup whipped cream
2 tbsp vanilla or rum extract;
*   or 1 tbsp Luzianne instant*
*   coffee and chicory*
2 tbsp butter
2 cups whole pecans
*   (preferably toasted)*

Pecan-studded pralines are a popular Creole treat.

A Superb Summer Sipper

The Southern Cosmopolitan, created by Susan and Tom Sully to com-
memorate Susan's book of the same title, is a local version of the famed
Cosmopolitan. Forego the martini glass and fetch the Mason jar (used
here as a cocktail shaker for preparation). Then pour into a chilled martini glass rimmed with a mint leaf and serve on a silver tray, of course!
To begin, combine two sprigs of mint, vodka, Cointreau, peach nectar,
and lime juice (quantities listed) with ice in a pint-sized Mason jar. Shake
vigorously then strain into the glass. Garnish with the remaining sprig of
mint. For the timid or teetotaler, I have included Susan's 'virgin' recipe.

THE SOUTHERN VIRGIN

Fill a Tom Collins glass with ice. Combine peach nectar, mint and lime
juice with ice in a pint-sized Mason jar. Shake vigorously then strain into
the glass and top off with club soda, stirring to mix. Garnish with the
remaining sprig of mint.

THE SOUTHERN COSMOPOLITAN
INGREDIENTS:

3 sprigs mint
1½ ounces peach-infused vodka
  (Absolut Peach)
½ ounce Cointreau
1 ounce peach nectar
¼ ounce fresh lime juice

THE SOUTHERN VIRGIN
INGREDIENTS:

3 sprigs of mint
2 ounces peach nectar
¼ ounce fresh lime juice
chilled club soda

Pots de Crème Please!

In New Orleans, serious Francophiles who entertain boast at least one
set of vintage porcelain *pot de crème* cups, the petite egg-shaped cups used
for custards. The French Creoles arrived in Louisiana with their services,
which explains their frequent appearance in the windows of the city's
best antique shops. In fact, Thomas Jefferson was besotted with a *Vieux
Paris* set while serving as the American Ambassador to France, and later
shipped the small cups to Monticello, his Virginia estate, where they are
displayed today.

The drama that surrounds any *pot de crème* presentation worth its cho-
lesterol is sometimes just the fun of what's inside. Our uptown friends,
Dr. Quinn Peeper and Michael Harold, own several sets of the delicate
porcelain cups and are experts at filling them. Serving them passed on
chargers or presented as a single dish, their *pots de crème* are a hallmark
of their homemade suppers. The filling for the pot de crème cups (the
plural, *pots de crème*, refers to both the cup and its filling) is a simple
custard (cream thickened with egg yolks). Flavors are virtually unlimited;
the custard is a blank canvas waiting for the inspiration of liquor, fruit,
vegetables, or even fish. Here, Quinn and Michael have provided four
recipes – one seafood, one savory, one sweet, and one laced with liquor. A
number of their choices were adapted from *www.potsdecreme.com*.

CRAB *POTS DE CRÈME*

In parts of South Louisiana, there are 'crab men' like 'Mister Louie' who lives in New Orleans and makes neighborhood rounds, dropping off orders of the freshest lump crabmeat available. Even without home delivery, crab in New Orleans is cheap, plentiful and can be purchased fresh year-round.

INGREDIENTS:

1 quart half and half
16 oz container of fresh shelled crabmeat (not jumbo lump because it is too clunky)
8 whole eggs
1 tbsp of butter
1 tbsp of olive oil
1 tbsp chopped garlic
1 tbsp minced ginger
1 tsp fish sauce (Nam Pla)
2 tbsp soy sauce
2 tbsp chopped Thai basil
2 tsp salt
1 tsp of Tabasco Sauce
1 tsp of white pepper
1 dozen shrimp shells (optional)

Simmer the half and half over low heat. To provide more flavor, you can add some of the discarded shrimp shells. Strain and cool the cream. In a separate pan, sauté the minced garlic and the ginger for 3 minutes until slightly browned. Transfer to a bowl and mix in the eggs, fish sauce, soy sauce, basil and salt. Fold in 14 ounces of crabmeat at the last minute, reserving approximately 2 ounces of crabmeat for the topping.

Gently ladle the mixture into shallow *pot de crème* cups and bake in a water bath at 300 degrees until set. Position the pots on the bottom of a deep baking pan. Pour warm water from a teapot into the pan covering half of the pots. The mixture should seem slightly 'wiggly' in the center. Remove from the water bath and serve warm or chilled.

Before serving: Clip chives on top of the mixture and add reserved crabmeat and a last squeeze of lemon juice for the topping.

TOPPING:

fresh chives
lemon juice

SAVORY POTATO & CAVIAR *POT DE CRÈME*

This potato recipe is the easiest to make and is heavy on presentation versus flavor. There are no precise measurements and the potato salad can be pre-purchased. If you are in a pinch for time but want a nice appetizer, this recipe is the best. No baking or water bath (bain marie) is required.

INGREDIENTS:

cold potato salad or mashed potatoes
caviar
crème fraiche or sour cream
lemon juice
truffle oil

Fill the individual *pot de crème* cups with potato salad ¾ full. Top with a dollop of either crème *fraiche* or sour cream and a heaping spoonful of caviar. Squeeze a few drops of lemon juice on top. Keep chilled and serve. The combination of potato and caviar provides a nice flavor. To make an over-the-top version, add a dash of truffle oil on top of the potato salad for more flavor. This version may be served with, or without lids.

Serves 8 - 10

TANGY POTATO SALAD

Boil potatoes until done, roughly about 20 minutes. Remove the skin and mash. Add the mayonnaise mixture and whip until smooth. Mash into the individual *pot de crème* cups and chill. Serve with lids.

Serves 8 to 10

INGREDIENTS:

1 pound potatoes
¼ cup chopped chives
¼ cup chopped parsley
½ tsp of curry powder
¼ tsp of celery salt
1 good splash of white wine
¼ cup mayonnaise
1 tsp of lemon juice
¼ tsp of salt
¼ tsp of pepper

POTS DÉ CHOCOLAT

Many of the pot de crème recipes call for a custard that is baked in a water bath, also called a 'bain marie.' This dessert one is an easy version that is made in a blender and chilled. It can be made within minutes and has a nice chocolate flavor. Use either dark rum or crème de menthe *to enhance the flavor.*

Put chocolate morsels in a blender and blend for 10 seconds. Scoop the sides and blend for a few seconds more. Add the hot water and blend for another 10 seconds.

Add egg yolks and blend for another 10 seconds. Meanwhile, in a separate bowl, beat the egg whites until fluffy. Pour and fold the egg whites and add rum or the *crème de menthe*. Spoon into the *pot de crème* cups and chill for 2 hours.

INGREDIENTS:

1 cup or one 6 oz bag of
   semi-sweet chocolate morsels
5 tbsp of boiling water
4 eggs
2 tbsp of dark rum or crème de
   menthe *for a minty flavor*

GRENADINE *POT DE CRÈME*

This can be served as a dessert with chocolate on the side or as a palate cleanser between courses. Either way, the pink color is a pleasant surprise when the lids are removed with a flourish, of course! Grenadine also has its origin in the pomegranate. (You can also add a little pomegranate juice for an extra bite.)

Mix two cups of buttermilk with the lemon juice, sugar, lemon zest, rum and corn syrup. Freeze until slightly mushy (under two hours). Place mixture in a cold bowl and beat smooth, adding grenadine. Gently ladle the mixture into 12 *pot de crème* cups and return to freezer until firm. Garnish with mint leaves.

INGREDIENTS:

2 cups of buttermilk
¼ cup lemon juice
½ cup of sugar
1½ cups clear corn syrup
½ cup Grenadine
1 tsp of lemon zest
1 tbsp of dark rum
mint leaves (optional)

Antique gilt *pots de crème* are stacked atop their matching "mazza" stand.

Quinn's Cooking Tips for *Pots de Crème*

1 The smaller the *pot de crème* cup, the faster the cooking time (be prepared to adjust cooking time when using different cups).

2 'Bake until set' means either: a) a toothpick inserted into the custard should come out clean; or b) the custard is firm around the edges, but still soft in the center.

3 Overcooking leads to a curdled texture resembling scrambled eggs.

4 Develop a garnish preference as your dessert *pot de crème* signature. Use a narrow spoon (an iced tea spoon is perfect) to top with whipped cream. Or add berries – black, blue, raspberries. Mint sprigs are nice, and chocolate-coated coffee beans add texture.

5 Lay a dishtowel on the bottom of the *bain marie* (water bath pan) to keep the cups from floating when in transit from the oven to the counter top.

6 Use a turkey baster to insert the custard into the cups. If needed, clean the edges of the cups with a paper towel before baking – otherwise, baking will solidify any spills. Once baked, it will not come off for the presentation.

Sweet & Savory: Shrimp & Strawberries

Because I love homemade biscuits, I've included two recipes – one sweet, one savory – topped with two local specialties, Ponchatoula strawberries and succulent Louisiana shrimp, respectively. Both recipes were given to me by my favorite New Orleans caterer, Joel Dondis.

CHEDDAR BISCUITS WITH GULF SHRIMP AND CREOLE *MEUNIÉRE* SAUCE

GULF SHRIMP
INGREDIENTS:

16 shrimp
½ cup canola oil
1 tbsp Creole seasoning
½ tsp salt
¼ tsp black pepper
2 tbsp butter
1 cup chopped green onion
½ cup chopped parsley

CHEDDAR BISCUITS
INGREDIENTS:

2 lbs flour
2 tbsp sugar
2 tsp salt
8 tsp baking powder
20 oz. cold, diced butter
2 and ⅔ cup milk
6 oz. shredded cheddar cheese

BBQ SHRIMP SAUCE
INGREDIENTS:

2 cups Worcestershire sauce
2 cups water
16 shrimp shells from the peeled shrimp
1 juice of a lemon
4 garlic cloves
½ cup diced onion
2 tbsp Creole seasoning
1 cup cream
3 tbsp butter

For Gulf Shrimp: Peel shrimp and reserve shells for sauce, below. Marinate shrimp in Creole seasoning, salt, black pepper and canola oil. Set aside to marinate for 30 minutes.

For Cheddar Biscuits: Sift together first four ingredients into a stainless steel bowl. Work in cold butter with pastry cutter until some small chunks remain. Add cheddar cheese and mix. Add milk and mix into a wet, sticky dough. Spread dough on heavily-floured surface to about 1½ inch thickness. Using a round pastry cutter, punch out 2½ inch circles and place on a cookie sheet. Bake at 350 degrees for about 20 minutes turning pan around halfway though. Let cool, serve (they freeze very well).

For BBQ Shrimp Sauce: Combine all ingredients except the cream and butter in a stainless steel sauce pot over medium. Reduce until approximately one cup of mixture remains. Add cream and reduce until sauce is thickened. Set aside.

To finish dish: Preheat oven to 325 degrees. Bring sauce to a simmer and whisk in butter until fully blended. Keep warm but be careful not to boil. Put 2 tablespoons of butter in a medium sauté pan set over medium heat. Once the butter has stopped foaming, sauté the shrimp, about 1 minute on each side. Top warm biscuits with two shrimp and a generous amount of BBQ sauce. Garnish with chopped green onions and parsley.

Gulf shrimp, a year-round delicacy, are served in a fancy version with *meunière* sauce on a bed of cheddar biscuits.

STRAWBERRY SHORTCAKE (BISCUITS)

Fresh Ponchatoula strawberries make a fabulous dessert when served as a topping for shortcakes, or even biscuits. Serve with what we call a 'hard sauce,' meaning a whipped cream with a dash of spirits – in this case Grand Marnier. It looks festive, and reminds me of summer in the South. Delicious!

Preheat oven to 350° F. Combine flour, sugar, baking powder, baking soda and salt in a mixing bowl and mix. Add cold butter and mix on medium low speed until it resembles coarse crumbs, about 3-5 minutes. Add buttermilk slowly until combined. Place dough on floured surface and gently roll out to 1-inch thickness. Cut into 2¼ inch circles with cookie cutter and place rounds onto sheet pan covered with parchment, leaving 2 inches between each shortcake. Gather together all remaining dough scraps and roll out and cut as above. Brush tops of shortcakes with buttermilk, then sprinkle with sugar. Bake for 10-12 minutes, turning pan halfway between baking time. Cool on baking rack.

Combine strawberries, vanilla, brown sugar and Grand Marnier together in bowl and fold gently with spatula. Set aside in cooler. Combine heavy cream and powdered sugar in mixing bowl and whip on high speed to stiff peaks. Refrigerate.

Cut each shortcake in half horizontally and place ½ cup of strawberry mixture, then ½ cup whipped cream, on each bottom half. Place top half on top of each shortcake. Dust with powdered sugar.

Serves 8

SHORTCAKES
INGREDIENTS:

2 cups all purpose flour
3 tbsp sugar, plus extra
*   for sprinkling*
1½ tsp baking powder
¾ tsp salt
½ cup butter, cold and
*   cut into 1 inch pieces*
½ cup buttermilk, plus 2 tbsp
*   extra for brushing*

STRAWBERRIES
INGREDIENTS:

4 cups Ponchatoula strawberries,
ends removed and cut into quarters
1 vanilla bean scraped gently
*   for seeds only*
½ cup brown sugar
¼ cup Grand Marnier
3 cups heavy cream
3 tbsp powdered sugar,
*   plus extra for dusting*

CRAB MAISON

Gently pick the crab apart to take out pieces of shell, making sure not to break up the large lumps, then place crab in a bowl. Season crab with salt and pepper and fold in the maison sauce. Clean, wash and pat butter lettuce dry, leaving the leaves whole. Place a bed of lettuce on each salad plate and top with crab salad; garnish with fresh chopped herbs. This can be served immediately or you can add one or all of the optional garnishes.

INGREDIENTS:

2 lb jumbo lump crab meat
2 heads butter lettuce
1 recipe maison sauce (right)
chopped parsley/tarragon/chives

OPTIONAL GARNISHES:

sliced radishes
sliced cherry tomatoes
grilled French bread croutons
lemon wedges

Two household favorites include a crab salad and a locally-baked Hubig's pie.

MAISON SAUCE

INGREDIENTS:

1½ cup canola oil
2 egg yolks
1 tbsp Creole mustard
1 tbsp lemon juice
2 tbsp white wine vinegar
1 hard boiled egg, sieved
2 tbsp diced shallots
1 tbsp capers chopped
2 tbsp parsley chopped
1 tsp tarragon chopped
1 tbsp chives chopped
2 anchovy filets chopped
salt
black pepper

Combine egg yolks, lemon juice and vinegar in a food processor. Add canola oil in a slow stream until it reaches a thick emulsion. Transfer to bowl and fold in remaining ingredients. Season with salt and pepper and refrigerate for at least two hours.

Ask me what my favorite dish is and I'll tell you flat out, "Anything cooked in New Orleans."

— Charmaine Neville

Pudding on the Ritz

Homemade banana pudding was always a childhood favorite, lovingly whipped up by my paternal grandmother, Ruth, for Sunday dinner (which, in South Alabama parlance, translates to lunch; dinner was a mid-day affair and supper was the last meal of the day). In reality, the dish was a version of trifle, a heavenly confection of custard, fruit, sponge cake and whipped cream, that has both English and French roots. When I wanted to dress up the basic recipe for parties, taking the dish from a simple pudding to a fancier trifle, caterer Joel Dondis perfected it for me. Below is his tasty version, which includes both bananas and strawberries (and a dash of rum), and looks as though Marie Antoinette would have included it among the French delicacies served at Versailles.

Creole trifles are still sold today in New Orleans' bakeries, and include all flavors of leftover cakes doused with rum or red wine, a sweet syrup or fruit juice and served chilled.

BANANA PUDDING TRIFLE

INGREDIENTS:

6 cups heavy cream
3 cups whole milk
1 split vanilla bean
   with seeds scraped
12 egg yolks
1 cup flour
2¼ cup sugar
1 cup banana liquor
2 tsp rum
12 ladyfingers (or sponge
   cake sections)
6 sliced ¼ inch thick, ripe bananas
3 tbsp powdered sugar
1 cup sliced ¼ inch
   thick strawberries

Combine 3 cups of heavy cream, milk, vanilla (seeds and pod) and salt in a heavy-bottomed saucepan and bring to a simmer. Meanwhile, cream the yolks, flour and sugar in the bowl of a mixer with a paddle attachment on medium speed. Strain the milk mixture through a fine mesh strainer, and then temper the eggs by adding to the yolk mixture in a slow steady stream with mixer on low speed until combined.

Pour egg-milk mixture back into saucepan, add ½ cup banana liquor and cook on medium heat, stirring constantly with wooden spoon, until mixture becomes thick and pudding-like in consistency. Be careful not to burn the mixture, especially on the bottom of the pan. Remove the mixture from heat, put banana pudding into a bowl and place a piece of plastic wrap directly on top of the pudding to prevent film from forming. Cool in refrigerator.

To make the whipped cream, combine remaining 3 cups heavy cream with powdered sugar in bowl of mixer and whisking on high until stiff peaks form. Remove from bowl and set aside in refrigerator. Make soaking liquid for ladyfingers by combining ½ cup banana liquor and 2 tsp rum in a shallow bowl long enough to hold a single ladyfinger horizontally. When pudding has cooled completely, assemble the trifle: Place a layer of banana pudding at the bottom of the trifle bowl to about 1 inch high. Place a layer of whipped cream on top of the pudding to about 1 inch high. Dip the ladyfingers, one at a time, in the soaking liquid, dipping each side. Place ladyfingers vertically all along the perimeter of the trifle bowl, leaving enough space in between each to fit a slice of banana. Push the bottoms of the ladyfingers into the pudding and whipped cream layers to support it. Place 2 banana slices vertically on top of each other, then a slice of strawberry in between each ladyfinger. The banana and strawberry slices, as well as the dipped ladyfingers should be up against the glass of the trifle bowl.

Now add a layer of sliced bananas on top of the whipped cream layer. Continue to build the trifle by putting a layer of pudding, then whipped cream, then bananas all the way to 1 inch from the top of the trifle bowl, while also continuing to place 2 slices of banana then one slice of strawberry in between the lady fingers all along the perimeter to 1 inch from the top of the trifle bowl. Place a layer of banana pudding at the very top of the bowl and then alternate slices of banana, then slices of strawberry horizontally all along the top's perimeter. Cover top of trifle with plastic wrap and cool in refrigerator.

Serves 8

Huîtres: Viva la difference!

Culinary heaven, to me, is a daily menu served on the half shell. I often think of the French writer Colette and her passion for truffles. "If I can't have too many," she said, "then I'll have none." Ditto for oysters! And, thankfully, New Orleanians share my passion. Being so plentiful here, oysters are a main ingredient in many local dishes and may be served simply – raw, steamed, grilled or dressed to the nines as, Oysters Rockefeller, a dish invented at Antoine's. To this day, Oysters Rockefeller is still a menu specialty there, but the actual recipe is a family secret and the folks at Antoine's refuse to part with it. Not to worry: I have included two easy recipes which are personal favorites, one plain, the other fancy. They are the buttery, bacon-flavored oyster stew that our friend George Massey makes every Thanksgiving, and the simple marinade he puts out for us during pre-supper cocktails. The latter is as easy as emptying a pint of oysters, liquid drained, into the mixture below. Skip the shell and go, oyster forks in hand, for the ones swimming in this rose-colored vinaigrette.

David Halliday presents two still-life studies in fruit.

GEORGE'S OYSTER STEW

Cut bacon into 1-inch pieces. Cook in a deep skillet until crisp, then extract from pan and set aside, leaving bacon grease. Add ½ stick of butter to grease, chop onions and add to skillet. Cook until clear over medium heat. Drain oysters and add to skillet with cooked onions (turn heat to medium low). Cook until edges of oysters start to curl. While oysters are cooking, add to mixture ½ teaspoon pepper, dash of salt, and two large dashes of Tony's seasoning. Add two tablespoons of Italian seasoning and just before the oysters curl completely, add the bacon back into mixture. While this is cooking, in a deep pot melt the rest of butter (½ stick) on low heat and add all of the half and half. Once oyster mixture is done, pour into half and half mixture and stir. Continue to heat over low heat until mixture is hot. Note: be careful not to overheat.

1 stick butter
8 pieces thick sliced bacon
1 medium onion
2 quarts oysters in liquid
½ gallon half-and-half
salt
pepper
Tony Chachere's Creole seasoning
Italian seasoning

I like to prepare this dish in advance and put into a crockpot (on low) after the mixture is hot. Then when guests arrive, it's ready to serve. You may serve informally by passing around in small demitasse cups or, for sit-down service, in large bowls.

OYSTERS MARINADE

Mix the marinade ingredients together in a covered dish and refrigerate for 2-3 hours. When ready to serve, drain oysters and place on oyster plate. Spoon a tablespoon of marinade onto oysters and serve with oyster forks. For a less formal serving, sans oyster plates, pour the marinade over the oysters in a serving bowl and then place on cocktail plates with a slotted spoon.

1 cup apple cider vinegar
⅕ cup red wine vinegar
1 tbsp lemon juice
1 tbsp coarse black pepper
¼ tsp minced garlic
1 shallot, grated
1 pint raw oysters (shucked and sealed in liquid)

Concocting the Crescent City Elixir

Spritz! Don't swallow! A non-edible recipe for 'cool'.

Summer is one of my favorite seasons in New Orleans, despite the oft-dreaded trio of heat, humidity and an occasional hurricane warning. Staying cool is, first and foremost, a mental exercise: think 'cool' and you are 'cool'. Remember to walk only on the shady side of the street. Cool your bare feet on the brick floor of the nearest court-yard garden. Sip 'spiked' lemonade. Wear a pretty linen sundress topped by a jaunty straw hat. Compose cold suppers of Creole tomatoes topped with lump crabmeat. Schedule long (and tepid) afternoon showers just before a 'siesta' summer nap. And always carry a purse-size spritzer of the *Crescent City Elixir*. New Orleans artist Amanda Talley created the brew, which she calls her 'cool down concoction' and happily shares the recipe below. The proportions can change depending on one's preferences for peppermint, rose water, clove, sandalwood or eucalyptus. The peppermint and eucalyptus cool the skin down while the oil keeps it moisturized, and the almond oil provides a glistening finish. Fill the nearest empty perfume bottle with the liquid and spritz away – or use generously as an *aprés-*shower splash.

Crescent City Elixir

3 parts almond oil
2 parts rose water
6 drops of peppermint oil
6 drops of eucalyptus oil
2 drops of clove oil
2 drops of sandalwood
(shake before each use)

SIX *Streets of Desire*

New Orleans' nickname, 'The Crescent City,' comes from the curling shape she takes as she hugs a bend in the Mississippi River. The large body of Lake Pontchartrain, with its neighboring cypress swamps, cradles her backside. Half-land and half-water, the city is neither island nor peninsula, but rather a plot of earth where geography dictates destiny at the base of America's most famously trafficked river. Roughly sixty percent of the country's dry goods float past her skyline as they travel south toward the Gulf of Mexico.

The city's watery boundaries have for centuries separated her not only geographically, but also culturally, from the 'other' America. She has birthed her own music: jazz and its siblings, zydeco, funk and blues. She is a second Paris; founded by French fathers, traded to and then reclaimed from Spaniards, cultivated early on by this heady mix of Europeans, and later populated by Africans and Caribbean peoples. New Orleans is a melting pot overflowing with a jambalaya of visibly-blended cultures; in her cuisine, her music and her people, one can literally see America's future.

The city's diverse cultural footprint is most palpable to me whenever I cross Canal Street, the city's main east-west boulevard and the great divide between 'uptown' and 'downtown.' Named both for its generous width, and plans for an aqueduct never built, I amuse myself with the irony: only a city bordered by great bodies of water would name a major thoroughfare after a canal. A century ago, it separated the Creoles, the first-born generation of arriving French (and sometimes Spanish) citizens, from those migrating South from Europe and the Americas. Today, locals still refer to "the French side" and "the American side."

Within the Garden District and the French Quarter, with their patchwork grid of smaller residential cross streets, New Orleans is a city best navigated by foot. Once inside these older neighborhoods, suddenly I feel immersed in a true 'walker's city,' rich in architecture, and richer

A European painting of a cherub is reflected in a Rue Royal shop window.

It has nurtured a great many people who live tolerably, like to talk and eat, laugh a good deal, manage generally to be civil and at the same time mind their own business.

—Walker Percy

still in ambience. Something about the confluence of French, Italian and Spanish architecture in these beautifully turned out neighborhoods transforms the intrepid traveler into what the Europeans call a *boulevardier* or *flâneur*, someone who strolls or promenades. New Orleans, like Paris, infuses a walk or a word with grandeur; in elevating the mundane to the marvelous, both never fail to lift the spirit. Thanks to Tennessee Williams' prosaic ode, everyone here knows of a street named Desire, but there is also Mystery, Music, Pleasure and Piety.

Ten blocks from my front door, on the opposite side of Canal, resides a reinvigorated Warehouse District. Formerly a cluster of abandoned warehouses, the neighborhood had the great good fortune to be considered an eyesore precisely when the city wanted to look its best for the 1984 World's Fair. A timely renovation followed. Today, the Warehouse District is a lively Soho-like enclave populated by newer condos, cafés and restaurants, small music clubs, and galleries that line the nexus of New Orleans' art scene at Camp and Julia Streets. It's the 'it' destination for those who love the juxtaposition of 'new' in an old city.

The city's true 'Main Street' is situated farther uptown: the part-residential, part-commercial Magazine Street is a bustling thoroughfare of residential Creole cottages and townhouses interspersed with retail shops, antique stores, cafés serving the city's signature 'po' boy' sandwiches, sno-cone stands and small grocers. Thriving local designers and decorators have made the street a national Mecca for those prowling for French and other European furnishings, antique silver and European-inspired décor with a Southern accent. The influence of Europe – all periods – is felt all over the city, but Magazine Street is its commercial heart. For interior design enthusiasts, there is more delight per square yard here than there is brocade in all of Paris.

Continue past Magazine Street, through the venerable Garden District, once a collection of plantations, now a more urbanized colony famous for its long stretches of mostly Greek Revival townhouses, Victorian cottages and Antebellum mansions. Its elegant historic structures look like a *mélange* of ornate wedding cakes, mostly white and pastel, sitting, in various sizes, on uniformly green lawns. The Garden District is bordered by the broadly paved streets of St. Charles Avenue, famous for its streetcar line, which began running in 1835 and is said to be the oldest of its kind in the United States. The avenue is flanked by clusters of tall magnolia trees mingling with large oaks, some trailing Spanish moss.

On the neighboring side of the French Quarter, a brisk walk downriver leads me to Faubourg Marigny, simply called "The Marigny" by locals. Here, cottages and shotgun houses – one-story dwellings without halls and easy to 'fire a shotgun through' – stylistically mirror their counterparts in the *Vieux Carré*. Today's Marigny bustles with small diners, second-hand bookstores, 'mom and pop' shops and the famed music clubs of Frenchmen Street. This is where Ellis Marsalis, Dr. John, and before them, Professor Longhair, pounded piano keys as they improvised and immortalized scat runs, trilling and filling the sultry night air with the songs that are now America's jazz, rum-boogie, or blues standards.

And then we come to my neighborhood, the place I knew was home before we ever had an address. New Orleans' *Vieux Carré* or 'Old Quarter' is a stage set of scenery "laced with miles of wrought-iron and lit by forests of gas lamps," wrote Walker Percy in his literary love ballad, *Mon Amour New Orleans*. The Mississippi's broad, scenic, curling river and its layers of French, Italian, Spanish, African and Caribbean culture, all intertwine, with lush tropical foliage and stark sunlight reminiscent of the South of France. Its period 18th- and 19th-Century architecture seems to come alive with a diverse, robust street *tableau* of locals, street performers, vendors, neatly-uniformed waiters, shop owners and cross-dressers, plus a constant flow of tourists parading in and around the high-spirited chaos. If I stand in a fixed spot out of the way and look at the big picture of humanity in motion, I am sometimes faced with a mirage of conga lines forming before me.

On most days, the Quarter is slow to rise after playing host to the latest long, celebratory evening in its trove of bars, cafés, bistros and restaurants. Tennessee Williams wrote about these "innocent mornings on Bourbon Street," where the first stealth sliver of daylight invades the silence. When the bustle finally does begin, mid-morning, waiters wear-

ing vests and carrying their newly-pressed tuxedo jackets make their way to work. The cooks follow in uniformed white garb. As in Paris, noisy garbage haulers mark the dawn with the first of their twice-daily clean-ups of every Quarter block and sidewalk, calling to each other as they sweep and spray a lemon-scented wash on the pungent streets. Like so many other scents in New Orleans, I have yet to sniff its lemony-mist in any other city in the world.

Still, for hordes of tourists, Bourbon Street is the city's most famous attraction. Most of it is chock-full with bars, strip clubs and tourist shops hawking t-shirts, masks and the 'only-in-New-Orleans' ingredients that can make even the most basic home cook feel like a sous chef: bottles of Avery Island's Tabasco Sauce, Creole spices, chicory coffee and *beignet* mix. But beyond the touristy commercial madness lies a quiet, residential stretch of quintessential New Orleans architectural styles that sit upon mostly silent streets with only a few shops catering to residents. Still, even in these quiet pockets, a steady jam of street sounds punctuate the peace within walled courtyards. Street life here is so evocative, so lively, that every interior space – the corner bar, the cathedral, the leafy court-yard garden – seems to offer the contrast of quiet sanctuary, shade from the strong sunlight, and a filter through which the church bells, jazz sounds and tourists' chatter are fused and buffered into a low, humming chorus.

I love the constant sounds, the music and the church bells. I never wear a watch any more because everywhere I go there are church bells ringing.

— Mary Matalin

Night sounds are the loudest, as they almost always involve revelry, including the shouts and shrieks of lost tourists, too many cocktails later, as they attempt to search for cars parked long-ago. Even New Orleans' seasons can be tracked by ear; in spring and summer, when tropical heat mixes with the almost-daily approach of rainstorms. I can hear the rain pounding on sidewalk pavements, splattering on tin roofs, tap-ping against large palm fronds, and the swooshing sound that banana leaves make when soughing in the wind. With their daily, year-round riffs improvised by the trio of rain, wind and heat, most afternoons feel lulling and laconic. The humidity creeps into and over our house until it

The St. Louis Cathedral towers above the treetops in Jackson Square.

Spanish street markers and gingerbread finishes are familiar details in the *Vieux Carré*.

becomes palpable and spreads a layer of almost embraceable air over the city. That embrace can feel like a hug from an older relative: a little too close, a little too long, yet comforting at the same time; a personal affirmation that you, or I, belong to *that* relative. No true son or daughter of New Orleans demurs from a little familial wet heat, much as Californians receive earthquakes as tiresome but proximate uncles who always happen to show up at inconvenient times. With the humidity, New Orleanians got the relative who never goes home.

Tour guides weave their way through the Quarter's maze of weathered streets by day and night, their wild narratives of history, lore and legend setting the pace for wide-eyed packs of tourists, some atop horse- or mule-driven carriages, others on foot. They wind their way through traffic to reach the city's stories. No other city can 'out-story' New Orleans. While it's true that almost all Southern cities offer historic home and garden visits, New Orleans possesses a vast, eclectic menu of ghost, vampire, haunted, mystery, and swamp tours. It's a vacation in paradise for connoisseurs of long-ago plantation life, voodoo spells, jazz haunts and the former red-light district known as Storyville.

In a city where parades and festivals are as common as carnival beads, and costumes often *de rigueur*, it is not unusual to encounter an individual slathered in gold paint from head to toe, or one sprouting feathers, or someone fashionably cross-dressed as a long-ago matinee idol or cabaret legend. I have encountered Elvis, Liberace, and Judy Garland on my morning errand runs.

Part of the amusements for locals is hearing tourists mispronounce street names. They invariably announce their arrival not by their dress or accent – the city is already a melding of styles and voices from far-away places – but by their pronunciation, or rather mispronunciation, of streets like Burgundy (pronounced Burr-GUN-Dee), Carondelet (Caron-doe-LET) and Chartres (Char-TERS); never mind Tchoupitoulas (Chop-a-TOO-lis), a derivative borrowed from the Choctaw Indian tribe. French-sounding streets shed their Gallic pronunciations long ago, possibly when the town's very first tourist discovered burgundy wine and Burgundy Street in the same night.

Royal Street is where tourists staying at the legendary Hotel Monteleone first come face-to-face with large shop windows of pricey European antiques. Its showrooms sell an amazing array of sterling silver pieces nestled inside inlaid mahogany chests, fine French furniture, odd pieces of porcelain, pottery and china patterns, many of which were discontinued long ago. I can always count, year-round, on the group of musicians playing outside what used to be the A&P on Royal, now a grocery chain called Rouses. (In New Orleans, things are called by their original names, not the names of the things they became later.) A combo or quartet might be performing, depending on time of day, or day of the week. The space is rarely without music, even on rainy days. On weekends, Royal Street is closed to vehicles, and larger groups play; percussion sets now join the scene as the musicians move from sidewalk to center street. I never know what I'll hear; it might be Django Reinhardt-like gypsy sounds, first-generation blues or the pride of the city's own jazz makers, depending on who got to the A&P first. Their songs ring out for several blocks, until I reach the point where Royal Street meets Pirate's Alley near the courtyard garden behind the Cabildo, once a seat of Colonial government, now a museum. There, just as the music grows muffled and fades, scent quickly overtakes me. All the trees in this part of the Quarter seem to exhale deep, heady breaths of Confederate jasmine.

The largest and oldest magnolia trees shade the public areas of the Quarter, like the one-and-only public schoolyard on St. Peter, or the police station on upper Royal, both of which are sandwiched between residential townhouses and blocks of small shops. In spring, I choose walking paths that take me in the direction of the blooming buds. Standing in their shade, I covet their blindingly-white petals, which seem lit from overhead by the natural sunlight. I always linger underneath their large extended branches, some of which hang low enough to bring me eye level with a blossom of this Southern magnolia – that *magnolia grandiflora* – lovely to see, say and touch. Always, I am tempted to reach for the flowers, snap their blooms free and carry them home. But I hear my grandmother's voice, and know that stealing magnolias, even contemplating such an act, would be a true sin. I simply could not walk home, passing the eyes of my neighbors, the familiar face of shop owners, and the look of inquisitive tourists who might inquire how I happened across a fresh, fragrant bouquet on such a warm afternoon. The sin comes in stealing, no doubt about it, but also in transporting the stolen flowers for my sole – and yes, unlawful – enjoyment. And so, I choose to forego the fragrant scent that wafts from their centers. I admire them from afar, and console myself that, if I am patient, an uptown friend might stop by with a freshly cut bunch from their garden, wrapped in the dampened pages of that morning's *Times-Picayune*. Once unwrapped, with stems removed, they would require at least two large porcelain bowls (no bud vases!) filled with water. For a few hours, the floating vessels would expand, and their strong floral scent would fill our rooms with light and fragrance, and then fade into yellow, their heady vapor erased from our house.

Each neighborhood walk offers fleeting glimpses of the flora planted in private courtyards, and locked behind wrought-iron garden gates. I spy a row of rainbow pastel Caribbean colors on ancient wood and stucco houses. Some are newly-painted. Others wear the faded colors bleached by the dual decay of wind and rain. In places where the paint has cracked, I can see revealed even older hues from past lives. Broken sidewalks have long ago erupted from the growth of live oaks spreading their roots beneath the soil. Their large cracks and occasional crevices remind me of the oak-desecrated and dilapidated small town sidewalks of my youth. I skip over the broken concrete as though playing hopscotch with myself.

Eventually, I come to my favorite footpath by walking toward the Mississippi on St. Philip, crossing toward the river to Bourbon Street, then onto Royal to Ursulines. To get there, I pass voodoo shops, art galleries, a small flower shop, a couple of bars, and a French bakery. I pause on a timeless stretch of Old New Orleans, at the intersection of Ursulines and Chartres where I gaze at the ambrosial view of gardens, cathedrals,

A busy day along the *Vieux Carré*'s Rue Royal is reflected in an antiques shop window.

Street scenes in the *Vieux Carré* reveal colorful shutters, blooming branches and a view of Pirate's Alley. *Opposite:* Peter Patout's Bourbon Street courtyard is a petite tropical paradise.

historic houses and courtyards. I pass the manicured courtyard that borders the well-preserved grounds of Beauregard-Keyes House and cross the street just in front of the Old Ursuline Convent, with its formal French-inspired gardens. Even in good economic times, when the blight of encroaching tourism threatened to scar the old quarter's gentility and grandeur, lower Chartres remained the way one would have imagined it a century or so ago. It does still.

Half a block from Chartres Street, I peer through the tall green gates of my favorite hotel, Soniat House, into the leafiest, most picturesque courtyard for blocks, then head through the stalls of the French Market to the Mississippi River levee. I stroll along a sidewalk path paved along the river's edge facing Jackson Square. The 'Moonwalk,' as it is now called, looks toward the horizon, framed by the rolling river and steamboats on my left. On my right, the famed postcard view of Andrew Jackson rises up on horseback in his namesake square in front of St. Louis Cathedral. Odds are, a single horn player or a few ad hoc groupings of two or three musicians will be playing for tips as I make my way to the levees, day or night. Here, the scene is complete with horse- or mule-drawn carriages, bougainvillea, street lamps and the curly cast iron gates of the Pontalba Apartments flanking both sides of the square. To me, this is the very essence of the French Quarter. To trace these small paths and grand boulevards always reminds me that life's best journeys are taken not by air or sea or wheels on asphalt, but on foot. In my mind and heart, in the whole of New Orleans, all streets lead to desire.

SEVEN *Paris is the Mother of New Orleans*

In her vampire novels, Anne Rice called Paris "the mother of New Orleans." The City of Lights had given the Crescent City "its life, its first populace," she wrote. "It was what New Orleans had for so long tried to be."

Had I never visited Paris, the streets of New Orleans would have provided me with a faint dream of her. Inside the *garçonniére* of our *Vieux Carré* house, hangs a series of maps of Paris, carefully segmented, framed and arranged so that her grand avenues and small streets alike can be traced end-to-end, from east to west, north to south. Eight perfectly formed grids of connecting lines and ovals, triangles and squares visibly outline the heart-shaped city. Reading the French names on the map, I recognize streets, alley ways, bridges and boulevards not only by their Parisian names, but by their corresponding New Orleans addresses. Here along the Louisiana coast, they live on, their French-sounding names fractured by Americanized pronunciations.

The French arrived here first, paying tribute to kings, dukes, sons and saints, as they laid out and christened the streets of the old city, the *Vieux Carré*, in 1718. Bienville and Iberville streets pay homage to the city's two founders, the brothers Le Moyne (formerly known as Sieur de Bienville and Sieur de Iberville), who named their city to honor the Duke of Orleans. Today, the French saints are still represented here – St. Ann, St. Peter and St. Philip streets among them. Ursulines Avenue was named for the French nuns who traveled to the New World where they set up a school and orphanage on the very site where the Old Convent Ursuline, the oldest surviving structure in the Mississippi River Valley, stands today. She sits quietly, reverently, and is flanked by the formal gardens that blanket her lovely grounds.

On the map, I locate *Rue du Maine*, the major avenue near *Montparnasse* in the 14th *arrondissement*, and think of our own house on Dumaine Street, named for the duc du Maine, Louis XIV's illegitimate son. Our

Bite-sized macaroons from Sucre' on Magazine Street are served in the parlor.

house was built upon an empty plot surveyed and sold to a free man of color in the early 1700s. Old deeds from our lot, much copied with their margins askew and faded serifs, read like a French roll call. . . De Baulne, Carriere, Landreaux, Le Brun and Godchaux.

Next, I discover the *Rue de Toulouse*, bordering the northwest suburbs of Paris, and further west, the *Quai de Conti*, named for the same Prince de Conti; both are Parisian precursors to two neighboring New Orleans streets, Toulouse and Conti. Are Elysian Fields and Esplanade not somehow corruptions of the *Champs Élysées?* There are countless real and perceived associations to be made between the mother and offspring; the city's transmuted Frenchness lies at the very core of public and private life, too. It is not so much a borrowed style as it is a cherished bequest.

As a child of the South, I learned in my early history lessons that all Southern cities have European roots. Charleston, Richmond, and even Baltimore, are essentially English; but New Orleans is culturally embedded in France. Latins, not Anglo-Saxons, founded her. Charleston gave us rice; New Orleans added spice and served up jambalaya. Her underlying, very European philosophy is predictably "live and let live." Add the bon mot, "live it up," and The Big Easy shifts with perfect ease from *"laissez faire"* to *"laissez les bon temps roulez!"*

Street Names
*In Paris/*In New Orleans:

*Rue Dauphine/*Dauphine Street

*Quai de Bourbon/*Bourbon Street

*Pont Royal/*Royal Street

*Allée Du Canal/*Canal Street

*Quai de Conti/*Conti Street

*Rue Saint-Louis en l'Ile/*St. Louis Street

*Rue de Toulouse/*Toulouse Street

*Quai d'Orleans/*Orleans Avenue

*Rue du Maine/*Dumaine Street

To get to New Orleans you don't pass through anywhere else. That geographical location, being aloof, lets it hold onto the ritual of its own pace more than other places that have to keep up with the progress.

—Allen Toussaint

A map of Paris streets echos the names of New Orleans' *Vieux Carré*.

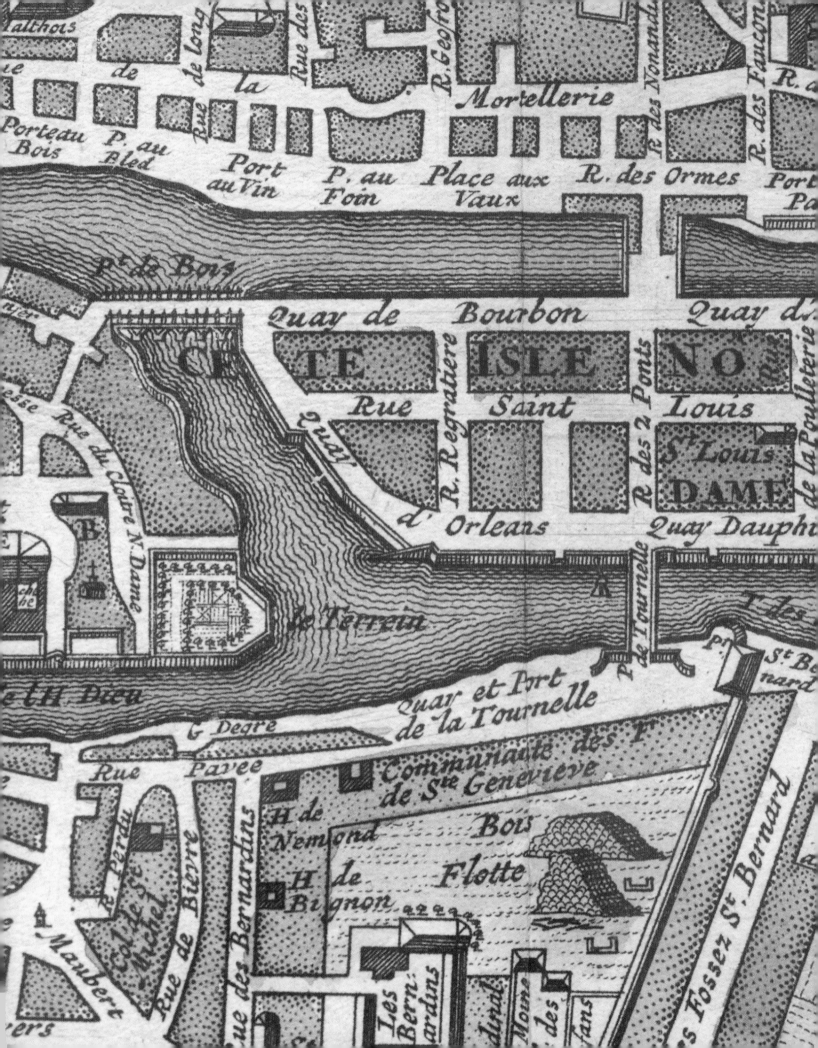

Chandeliers, one colorful and one a ghostly reflection, hang from the ceiling of Karla Katz and Co. on Magazine Street.

Traces of France appear in labels and ribbons and amid the weathered walls of
Napoleon House bar and café in the *Vieux Carré*.

Underneath her vibrant cultural mix, New Orleans' French heart still
beats. Signs of this Gallic allegiance are everywhere: in my morning *café
au lait* and *beignets* (French donuts) at the famous Café du Monde, the
oldest coffee establishment in America. Two blocks homeward lies the
open-air French Market, whose entrance is framed by a miniature *Arc de
Triomphe*. Another route takes me, always with the local *Times-Picayune*
in-hand, to the *Croissant D'Or*, a small patisserie a few blocks from home,
for a morning *pain au chocolat* and the day's fresh foot-long *baguette*. I
carry it home in its thin, white paper casing. A few hours later, I tear off
the ends to mop up the remains of watery roux from my gumbo lunch.
Sweeping the crumbs aside, I soak the leftover bread overnight in a
bowl of fresh milk before baking the following morning. The *baguette's*
remains are destined for one of the many decadent recipes for *pain perdu*,
or 'lost bread,' the city's Americanized version of a bread pudding. Some
recipes are flavored with chocolate, or whisky; almost all are made with a
generous dose of pecans and rum-soaked raisins. Most are sprinkled with
powdered sugar and served with ample whipped cream or an alcohol-
laced hard sauce, or all of the above. And, of course, no dessert in New
Orleans is complete without the bitter after-taste of the ubiquitous,
endive-based chicory coffee.

New Orleans never strays far from its founding French fathers, no matter the meal or the month. Evenings in high-end restaurants often begin with the traditional Parisian prelude: Champagne or a Champagne Cocktail in tall, faceted French flutes sold throughout the city's antique shops. It is said that the cocktail was invented here. But beyond the heavenly Sazerac, or the orange peel whiff of a Ramos Gin Fizz, there is a taste for *Lilette*, a French-bottled liquor whose homemade versions are sold from large glass jugs as *vin d'orange*. And then there is the city's drink particular, absinthe, nicknamed 'the green fairy.' Absinthe is served the old French way: glass apothecary fountains drip cold water over sugar cubes. The sugar water flows through perforated spoons that are balanced across glasses of the pale green liquid.

Parisian-style bistros, *brasseries*, *pâtisseries* and cafés are sprinkled like sugar granules throughout New Orleans Parish (America has counties, Louisiana has parishes). In older, more established restaurants, the first course is whisked from side-table to table by formally-dressed waiters who are trained in the service *à la Françaisé*. They wheel a cart of fish and fowl or fruit-laden dessert, all the while carving, garnishing and presenting its ingredients with a flourish for the diner (and everyone else) to see.

The Parisian influence on food and drink extends all the way to heaven; that is to say, desserts and sweets. Simply peer into the reflective glass cases of Sucré on Magazine Street. Inside, delicate stacks of pastel, French-inspired macaroons show off their fruity flavors. Their spherical shapes, shiny eggshell finish and nutty taste remind me of the counterparts sold at Ladurée in Paris. French versions of king cakes, a more festive and seasonal cousin of the apple *tarte tatin*, are still sold during Carnival, and shipped around the world to those with ties to a city that spends two months preparing for the *finale* of Mardi Gras.

Photographer Erika Goldring captures Buckwheat Zydeco's accordion.

The fingerprint of France is indelible here, even after nearly three centuries of New Orleans history layered atop it. The cultural adaptations are legion. For example, the French introduced masked balls in 1718. Today, the die-hard revelers of the old Carnival traditions don wax masks made in Paris, shunning the Venetian-made masks found in the city's souvenir shops. The *fleur-de-lis*, or French lily, the city's leitmotif, appears on everything from petit fours to gatepost finials. *Réveillon* dinners still recreate the traditional French Creole repasts just before Christmas. A cadence of pure French or a part-English *patois* is still spoken in corners of New Orleans, as well as in the nearby swampy bayou hamlets just south and west of the city, nearer to the Gulf of Mexico. I can hear French-sounding notes in the sweet night rhythms of an accordion player's lonely gypsy ballads. The joyous, raucously fast chords of zydeco first sounded in this area when French peasants, forced out of Nova Scotia's Acadia region in the late 1700s, settled in Louisiana.

Napoleona!

Although he never set foot upon New Orleans soil, never even sailed to America, the ghost of Napoleon Bonaparte is everywhere. He is city father in absentia, icon and overseer. Here, every school-age child is versed in the Louisiana Purchase, in which the Emperor sold New Orleans to America for just seven U.S. dollars in 1803. Napoleon's likeness, in either commanding profile or as a symbolic French bee, appears on fabrics, porcelain and paintings, as well as a seal upon campaign beds and other Empire period furnishings sold along Magazine Street. Uptown streets, Austerlitz, Jena, Marengo and Milan, Constantinople and Cadiz, bear names of his battlefield victories. And, Louisiana remains the only state among fifty to live under the Napoleonic Code, and not British Common law.

For both tourists and steadfast locals, the Emperor's lore lives on most visibly in Napoleon House, the famous shrine-cum-bar located at the corner of St. Louis and Chartres Streets. Built in 1797 as a private residence for New Orleans mayor Nicholas Girod, it overflows today with relics of Napoleon nostalgia, the most notable being an urban legend involving pirate Jean Lafitte. The two sympathizers, politician and pirate, planned to rescue the Emperor from exile and house him in the upstairs apartments. Alas, he died before 'The Plot,' as it is known locally, could be carried out.

A symmetrical display of shutters is arranged along a stucco façade of the Napoleon House, a Chartres Street Landmark.

The Lure of Linen Landscapes

New Orleans has its own classic twist on the French-inspired *toile de Jouy*, or *toile*, a classic single-color fabric of repeated images featuring beautifully drawn vignettes. The linen landscape depicts St. Louis Cathedral, the St. Charles street car, the steamboat Natchez, and the architecture of the historic *Vieux Carré*. Artist Sonia O'Mara based the design on original sketches by Bryan Batt, who sells yards of it in his Magazine Street shop, Hazelnut. It is printed in four romantic colors (tan, brown, red or blue – *non!*) – magnolia, *café au lait*, claret and delphine.

Pass the *Vieux Paris* Please!

What would service *à la Française* be without French porcelain? Some of the best tables in New Orleans are set with *Vieux Paris*, or 'Old Paris' tableware named for the hard-paste porcelain either made in early Parisian factories, or decorated (painted) in Paris. *Vieux Paris*, a favorite collectible among generations of New Orleanians, was popular among French Creoles who lived in the city's great houses and along the lower Mississippi River Valley. (Today, the New Orleans Museum of Art is the only place in America to house a complete survey of Old Paris). Inside a friend's Garden District kitchen, a simple French armoire houses a vast array of the classic white service with a gold band, or 'wedding ring' pattern that began with inherited pieces from the collector's grandmother. Additional pieces were purchased from local antique shops along Royal and Magazine streets.

Like every other tourist passing before me, I am charmed by Napoleon House. I came for the house drink, the cucumber-laced gin-infused cocktail known as the Pimm's Cup, and stayed for the ambience. The legend of The Plot may be just that, but the old three-story structure is as authentic a landmark as the pious grounds of nearby Old Convent Ursuline. The inner courtyard of Napoleon House resides, in both winter and summer, in a perfect chiaroscuro of half-shade, half-light. Palmettos feigning umbrella shapes frame its French bistro tables. Giant palm fronds fan crumbling walls whose chalky, mottled surfaces have been perfectly weathered by a trio of benign neglect: time, humidity and indifference. All have conspired to attract a constant flow of *trompe l'oeil* students who travel from Florence to marvel at the decay that two centuries can wreak upon plaster. As if it required a musical score to further heighten the allure, the management states clearly on it's thin, cheaply-printed menu that only classical music and opera shall be played – at the patron's request, of course.

Upstairs, *L'Appartement de L'Empereur*, along with the Salon de Josephine, a trio of airy rooms awash in the Empress' favored colors of pale blue and yellow, await the wide-eyed trespasser. At night, these connecting suites masquerade as a series of three *petite* ballrooms. Here, patrons drink and dance to old-time jazz orchestras who play period music during Carnival and Twelfth Night, or for small wedding parties who arrive via a 'second line' parade led by bride and groom from St. Louis Cathedral farther down Chartres Street.

Mon dieu! Monsieur Marcel!

In keeping with the Crescent City's connection to all things French, four well-known New Orleanians have taken a page from French novelist and celebrated writer Marcel Proust. A famous diarist, Proust carried a red notebook with gold embossed letters which read in English, *"Confessions, An Album to Record Thoughts, Feelings."* His notes, written in his native language, contain answers to the now famous Proust Questionnaire. Painter, musician, restaurateur and chef – all icons of the city – share their favorite meals, cocktails, neighborhoods, memories and obsessions. Turn the page and all will be revealed!

Shelves of Old Paris porcelain are stacked inside an antique French armoire in a Garden District home.

My New Orleans by *Ella Brennan*

Occupation: Restaurateur

The best thing about the city is: the people and the food.

My favorite meal is: freshly-caught flounder with fresh jumbo lump blue crabmeat with herbs and a light butter sauce.

My favorite cocktail is: a Sazerac or an Old Fashioned.

New Orleans is the only place in the world where: you'll see a jazz band coming down the street if you wait long enough.

My favorite neighborhood is: The French Quarter because it has fit into every era and it's a real walking neighborhood.

The city's most marked characteristic is: joie de vivre.

My favorite New Orleanian is: Lindy Boggs and Leah Chase because they are hard working ladies who enjoy New Orleans as much as I do.

If I had a free hour, I would spend it: sitting by my beloved Mississippi River.

My one New Orleans obsession is: eating and drinking and carrying on!

I knew the spell of the city had been cast upon me when: I was first old enough to have a *café au lait* and French bread for breakfast.

My New Orleans by *Chef Emeril Lagasse*

Occupation: Chef and Restaurateur

The best thing about the city is: the locals and the meals.

My favorite meal is: a fried shrimp po' boy.

My favorite cocktail is: a Sazerac.

New Orleans is the only place in the world where: food, people and music meld together magically.

My favorite neighborhood is: the Warehouse District because I like to think I helped pioneer it.

The city's most marked characteristics are: St. Louis Cathedral and the river.

My favorite New Orleanian is: Ella Brennan because she is a legend.

If I had a free hour, I would spend it: walking down Magazine Street checking out all the shops and galleries.

My one New Orleans obsession is: food!

I knew the spell of the city had been cast upon me when: I felt the combination of music, food and people in my soul.

My New Orleans by
George Rodrigue

Occupation: Painter

The best thing about the city is: it's an eclectic collection of people, architecture, art, music, and food.

My favorite meal is: K-Paul's potato salad because it's just like my mama used to make.

My favorite cocktail is: a Virgin Mary.

New Orleans is the only place in the world where: you can hide in public, becoming anyone you want on Mardi Gras Day.

My favorite neighborhood is: Faubourg Marigny because it's where I live with my family. It's a diverse collection of people of all ages and backgrounds and in some ways is a microcosm of the city as a whole.

The city's most marked characteristics are: French Quarter, streetcars, Garden District, Galatoire's, Café du Monde and Jackson Square.

My favorite New Orleanian is: Joe Segretta – to me he's a classic New Orleanian who grew up in the French Quarter and still loves the city. I stop by Restaurant Eleven 79 several times a week just to hear his stories.

If I had a free hour, I would spend it: looking at the Mississippi River, sitting on the back porch of my old Creole townhouse, watching the ships go by.

I knew the spell of the city had been cast upon me when: I was 12 years old, we would drive from New Iberia on the old Highway 90 and park right in front of Café du Monde for *beignets* and coffee-milk (as they called it back then). That was the beginning for me.

My New Orleans by
Wynton Marsalis

Occupation: Musician, Artistic Director of Jazz at Lincoln Center

The best thing about the city is: its colorful people.

My favorite meal is: gumbo.

My favorite cocktail is: the Caipirinha.

New Orleans is the only place in the world where: a Confederate general who abandoned the city could have the most prominent statue.

My favorite neighborhood is: Pigeon Town because that's where I'm from.

The city's most marked characteristics are: shotgun houses and raised cemeteries.

My favorite New Orleanian is: Louis Armstrong because he taught us all how to be natural and modern.

If I had a free hour, I would spend it: riding the loop.

My one New Orleans obsession is: have us learn and respect our culture.

I knew the spell of the city had been cast upon me when: I had a street parade in a suburb of New York attended by three people.

Gris-Bleu & Bleu-Vert

The rainbow colors of the *Vieux Carré* houses harmonize in such a way that all the streets seem to blend into one life-sized painted canvas. One block wears the palette of a Rothko, with its muddy pinks, clay reds and somber browns. One street over, Cezanne clearly created a colorful composition upon slices of stucco, starting with caramel and lilac, and ending with a ripe olive bordering a moody blue. On still another block, a Gauguin-themed scene of sun-saturated citrus shades of orange sit next to peach, and a Creole pink resides side-by-side with a Pontalba rose, in colors that could only have been inspired by the Mississippi River at sunset.

More than one enthusiast, paint knife surreptitiously in hand, has 'borrowed' a few contraband paint chips from favored houses; out of a handful of colored dust, stored and folded in paper envelopes for safekeeping, comes a delicate wash of pigment. Later, trim, hardware, shutters and doors will be painted a darker contrasting shade. In true 'Mrs. Blandings' fashion, green becomes either a French Quarter Green or a Paris Green depending upon the owner's sensibilities. Could they be one and the same? Or do these pigments reflect the bystander's eye, filtered through a romantic haze instead of a prism of pure sunlight?

The *Vieux Carré* Commission, which oversees the Quarter's historical continuity, mandates the colors of its buildings with great diligence. Yet, no actual color wheel exists. Those seeking approval to alter the shades of doors, windows, or walls are handed a two-page essay outlining four color periods that span a hundred years, roughly 1820 to 1920. First came pastels and whites; next, the Victorian era ushered in broader, deeper tones, followed by muted shades before a return, again, to the whites and silken pastels of a century ago. Today, vibrant French-Caribbean colors reign in the *Vieux Carré*. Farther away from the river, the unregulated, un-coded color configurations of neighborhoods, notably the Bywater and Treme, are bathed in *tres flagrante* shades: here, turquoise, lavender and lime cozy up to cornflower and cornelian blue.

Parisian silhouettes hint at the identity of master and mistress of the house.

Parisian Profiles Adorn the Parlor

Silhouettes of the master and mistress of the house (my husband and I!) adorn the antique *gris-bleu* bookcase in the master bedroom. These cut-out portraits cost just a few Euros and were made in a matter of minutes by a street artist working from a mobile studio overlooking the *Seine*. Since the term, silhouette, was first published in an 1835 French dictionary, the profiles make perfect Parisian souvenirs for displaying in a French Quarter home.

Two crimson collages illustrate Paris, the mother, and her offspring, New Orleans.

Traces of France are found in an Old Paris terrine and a French portrait peering between panels of ancient wallpaper.

Charting the Connected Cities

If Paris, the mother, is a refined courtesan, then New Orleans is her younger, sometimes wayward daughter. The mother's bridges flank the Seine; her daughter is anchored in the muddy riverbanks of the New World's Mississippi, which is slow-moving, yet more commercially important than its beatific Parisian counterpart. If Paris is the moon, New Orleans is the moon child. Paris may be, as Hemingway famously wrote, "a movable feast," but New Orleans is the effervescent cocktail, the *aqua vitae.*

There is little doubt the two cities are connected. Intuitive Michele Bernhardt looks at the birth charts of parent, Paris, and her offspring, New Orleans.

Paris celebrated the First Republic on September 26, 1792; that makes her a Libra. Libras are partner-oriented: their souls want to function in the 'we' consciousness (no pun intended). No wonder Paris is so romantic. Libra is an air sign. The city is surrounded by a forest of beech and oak trees, mainly along the *Bois de Bologne*, which purify the atmosphere (a good thing, since there is so much smoke in the cafes!).

Ruled by Venus, Paris is obsessed with all things refined and aesthetic. The symbol for Venus is shaped like a hand mirror, reflecting beauty, self-love, and vanity.

With the Moon in Aquarius, Paris is hip, innovative – and socially responsible (for example: five weeks' paid vacation is *de rigueur* for France's workforce). Mars in Scorpio in the first house explains why Parisians can be intense, proud, and stubborn. Mars rules speed and activity. Call it coincidence, but Paris is never dull, and the locals drive fast. With Scorpio rising, Paris is a place of mystery and passion. With Saturn opposing the ascendant, however, Parisians can be reserved when meeting someone new.

Leo rules the 10th house, making Paris a place of great ceremony. You expect the unexpected there; you feel intensely alive.

New Orleans and the moon have always seemed to me to have an understanding between them.

— Tennessee Williams

New Orleans was born (incorporated) on February 17, 1805 under the sign of Aquarius. Aquarians are known for being unique and progressive. This would certainly explain the city's cultural mix. It easily embraces newcomers and welcomes them from other parts of the world.

While Venus, the planet of love and beauty and feminine allure, influences Paris, New Orleans is ruled by both Uranus and Saturn, which celebrate a duality of male and female characteristics.

Uranus embraces the unusual, the individualistic and those who 'break the rules.' Saturn on the other hand is conservative in nature, has a resistance to change and a love of tradition. No wonder the city is such a dynamic mix of the old and the new.

Jupiter and Neptune are in the 6th house of health, daily routine, and work. Jupiter's love of excess and indulgence combined with Neptune's fondness for food and drink and the desire for escape make New Orleans a fun-loving place and give it no chance of being a spa diet destination. Dining here transports your senses. The result: no *gastronomique* structure, discipline or stability, and no rules allowed!

Neptune's aspect gives New Orleans' the urge to embrace the intangible and touch what one cannot see. With Mars in the sign of Leo, its people are creative, dramatic and expressive. Love affairs and romance figure prominently in the city's star chart, as does a desire for freedom and the unconventional.

The conjunction of the Sun and Pluto enhances the themes of sex, magic, power and transformation that so palpably live here. Death and rebirth are continual themes. New Orleans is poetic, talkative and witty with lively street performers and a host of celebrated jazz musicians. With Gemini rising, communication plays a vital role in this outgoing city. Her people are friendly. She attracts writers and artful conversation. The Moon in Libra only increases the city's hospitality and beauty. Here, one's home is one's castle.

There are many connections between these two enchanted cities on different continents. Their mirror identities may well be moonstruck: Paris is born under the Sun sign of Libra, which is where the Moon is in New Orleans' chart. And New Orleans is born under Aquarius which is where the Moon is in Paris's chart. The moon and moonchild understand each other in a deep and exotic way.

New Orleanians are not emulators.
They are individuals.

– Ella Brennan

A generous serving of morning *café au lait* arrives in a crown-emblazoned cup.

What your sign can hope to find in Paris. . . & in New Orleans

ARIES Will never be bored/
Will never resist the spell of the city

TAURUS Dinner at Maxim's/
Dinner at Commander's Palace

GEMINI Café crème & endless conversation/*Café au lait* & endless *beignets* (French donuts)

CANCER Secret hideaways/
Secret garden paths

LEO Romance/Unrequited longing

VIRGO An Hermes scarf/
A Krewe of Hermes *bal masque*

LIBRA Hand-holding/Fortune telling

SCORPIO Passion, mystery and dark corners/Sultry music played in half-lit clubs on dark streets

SAGITTARIUS History/Remembrance

CAPRICORN Great shopping and Champagne/Great antiquing followed by your choice of a Sazerac or Pimm's Cup

AQUARIUS A quiet subway system/
A quiet walk in the city's public gardens, be it Audubon, Armstrong or City Park

PISCES Chanel No. 5/
Night jasmine falling from the trees

EIGHT

The City of My Final Destination

Avez-vous voodoo?

There are not one, but two voodoo shops on Dumaine Street. The first voodoo ceremony in New Orleans is said to have occurred in the early 1800's in an abandoned brickyard a few blocks from our house. I find the presence of the shops, our street's history, the legacy of voodoo – all of it, curiously intertwined. Now, almost two centuries later, each night a line of tourists snakes past our front door en route to St. Louis Cemetery No. 1, on the edge of Basin Street. The faithful are making a pilgrimage to Tomb No. 347, the resting place of New Orleans' most celebrated voodoo priestess, Marie Laveau (ironically, if voodoo had a patron saint, it would be Laveau). The tale-spinning tour guides who lead transfixed groups through these 'cities of the dead' consider the tomb of 'Mam'zelle Leveau' to be the *ne-plus-ultra* of attractions. Visitors believe that inscribing a series of three small x's on the chalky white surface of her crypt will bring them good luck. Local authorities beg to disagree: they classify the markings as graffiti, an act of defamation, for the historic cemetery with its above-ground mausoleums.

These same 'ghost guides' claim that one in five New Orleanians practice voodoo. This is perhaps an exaggeration on the part of the eager tour guides who do their best to entertain and sometimes playfully spook their captive clientele. However, there is little doubt that New Orleans is America's voodoo capital. Voodoo practitioners – including the manbos, mambos, priestesses, root doctors, ancestral guides and queens – fall into two categories: the serious and the seriously commercial. All are quick to specify their expertise in a variety of voodoo forms, be it Haitian vodou, vodun, hoodoo, Louisiana voodoo and the very local 'New Orleans voodoo.' (Voodoo is like dialect here, with regional variations and local subtext.) 'Tourist voodoo,' as some skeptics call it, has been hugely commercialized throughout the *Vieux Carré*, given the number of shops selling gris-gris bags (carried to ward off danger), potions, powders and amulets. For better or worse, these tourist establishments have fed the mystique, keeping its history and practice alive.

A silent city of the dead leads to St. Louis Cathedral.

The banister curls skyward from a French Quarter stairwell. *Opposite:* Religious relics appear as sculpture.

It's true that I pass a voodoo shop more often than a book store here in the Quarter, as I go about my daily routine. Eventually, my curiosity leads me to a place I have passed a thousand times, just two blocks from our house. At first glance, Voodoo Authentica resembles a well-merchandised craft shop, except it sells, along with its vast array of powders and potions, literally dozens of the apparently quintessential voodoo dolls. They cover almost every wall, table and surface of the two-room shop. Some are larger and more elaborate than others, but almost all of these handmade effigies, no matter how primitive, wear a wrapped head cloth called a tignon. The dolls are surrounded by hand-crafted items including an array of small pouches, amulets and gris-gris bags (also called zinzins), which were the forerunners of the small leather pouches created by African medicine men to keep hunters safe.

Fingering the amulets, fetishes and pre-packaged powders concocted for very specific remedies, e.g., to cure toothaches, headaches and even heartaches, I can easily see how a prescribed ritual that involves meditating, lighting candles, pouring libations and feeding of spirits, would be a tempting means of solving all life's dilemmas. My one and only brush with the topic of sorcery so far had been during a brief, yet intense lunch conversation many years ago with a magazine editor in London's Haymarket Hotel. For a scarce (and scary) moment, we locked eyes, as she leaned in with a whisper to explain. Due to our fair skins, light-colored eyes and starkly premature grey hair, she said confidentially, we were both "white witches" imbued with magical powers. She named others in our common circle who fit the same physical (if not metaphysical) description, and then proceeded, without hesitation, to offer up a detailed and well-thought out scenario of our talents and identifying characteristics. But that was mere conversation, conjecture, and for her, confession; here, in my own neighborhood voodoo shop, all methods of rituals, rites, spells, meditations and incantations are sold with props, price tags and ingredients, as though they were common spices. First the mortar and pestle, and now the rosemary to grind.

Scanning one table of offerings, I bypass the more generic blessings for love, friendship, money, luck and success, and am immediately drawn instead to the more alluring, enigmatic 'Mistress of the House.' This, I learn from the shopkeeper, is an old spell, created by a woman known simply as 'Lady Veve' and sold for many generations to women seeking power, confidence and the ability to be "boss of their own lives." For just a few dollars, pennies per sorcering, I purchase the recipe, which is printed on parchment paper and sealed in a matching envelope by an irregular circle of red wax. The spell takes place over a nine-day period. This

Love Potion Number Nine

ATTRACTION OIL Mix equal parts rose, lavender, vanilla and sandalwood oils. Touch pulse points when in the presence of the object of your attraction.

LUCKY OIL Create mixture of ½ olive oil, ¼ myrrh and jasmine oils. Anoint feet before wearing shoes you will wear in situation where you desire luck.

POWER OIL Mix equal parts patchouli, cinnamon and vanilla oils. Touch wrists and temple area before entering situation in which you desire power.

PROTECTION OIL Mix equal parts hyacinth, jasmine, orange, musk and anise oils. Apply oil to areas that need protection. Apply to soles of feet to run away from evil.

A collection of pine cones, hats, knives and guns are arranged in an altar-like fashion.
Potions' source: http://users.erols.com/irene/voodoo.htm

Voodoo potions, gates and altars reference the "beyond."

involves, first, finding a purple glass container with a matching purple lid, then mixing into it nine tablespoons of jojoba oil with single tablespoons of coarse ground herbs, including calamus root, rosemary, black pepper, clove, fennel seed, lavender, ginger and thyme. The mixture sounds like an edible sauce or a tasty brew for a marinade, except for the last tea-spoon, which is a mysterious ingredient called devil's shoestring. Actually, although it sounds mystical, if not cabalistic, it is related to the honey-suckle vine. Its name comes from its imbued ability to 'trip up the devil.'

I must return to the shop to purchase the more exotic, non-household items, and, once there, I realize I've forgotten my list. So I ask again for the spell and am told by the same shopkeeper who sold it to me that no such item exists. I am baffled, and feel certain that I bought the spell at this shop, but I return home empty-handed, to try again. Days later, list firmly in hand, I revisit the shop to gather the ingredients. The scruffy but amiable shopkeeper uses his hands to measure the various herbs, twigs and seeds that I need, which he pours carefully from individual ma-son jars that he keeps in an antique glass pharmacy case. He sells them to me in small, individually sealed bags. A large jar of curry-colored powder catches my eye; its handwritten label reads, 'Red Brick Dust.' When I ask, the clerk tells me that the red substance is one of the more com-monly sold items. When mixed with soapy water, it is used to wash down the porch steps to keep evil or negative energy from entering a house.

I return home to prepare my own voodoo experiment. My spell recommends a Wednesday evening meditation at precisely nine o'clock and an offering of red wine and nine plums on an altar (my kitchen table), while burning lavender incense. I do all of the above, as I prepare the mixture, and choose a delicate purple flacon that once adorned my dressing table. It still contains faint traces of an intense tuberose scent called Fracas, a once hard-to-find cult French fragrance I had worn in my twenties. The metaphor of washing away the old traces of perfume and refilling the vessel with an elixir promising power and confidence is not lost on me; it feels like a rite of passage. I rinse the fragile violet glass, long empty but slightly stained from the residue of soft, caramel-colored fragrance, and fill it with the potion. I seal it with the glass top and leave it to sit in a cool, dark place (our kitchen pantry). Ironically, the date on the calendar is September 9, 2009 – a strange coincidence considering the timing of the spell was delayed because I misplaced the list of ingredients. And so, at 9 pm, on the ninth day of the ninth month, in the year 2009, I mix nine ingredients and wait the same number of days for the voodoo potion to set. On the last day, I remove the glass bottle, and apply the oil to pulse points on my wrist and neck. I resume my daily routine of neighborhood errands, a swim at a nearby pool, a walk with the dogs and a small lunch and a late supper involving friends, all with the sense of anticipation.

I believe in time. I believe in history. I believe in memory. I believe in the memory that ritual evokes.

—Patrick Dunne

Days and weeks passed. Months flew by. Nothing in my life had changed. I had looked for secret signs, both everyday omens and more defining and dramatic bodings that the voodoo that I had practiced alone and in my very own kitchen had taken hold. And then, I began to realize that our house already had a mistress. She was willful, fiercely protective, unyielding when crossed, and yet open enough to welcome kindred spirits, along with the 'spirited,' through the front door and into its rooms. She was me. No spell was needed. Providence, not potions, had prevailed. The universe had seen fit to give us the keys and then led us inside.

Long before I brought it into my kitchen, voodoo arrived in the Americas, and specifically, the banks of the Mississippi, aboard the first slave ships from Africa. It was the early 1700's and New Orleans was little more than a French colony. The slaves sold along Congo Square in New Orleans were forbidden to read or write, or gather in large groups. So, from the very beginning, voodoo in this country had underground origins. It thrived as a secret religion without church, canon or any consistent or written history. Today, it has many tribes. It is part-chameleon, part-old customs, changing in small ways to adapt to the times. Like so many other elements of New Orleans culture, in Darwinian fashion, it took key elements of established religions and cultures, and blended parts into a whole to survive. A local manbou tells me that as owners converted slaves to Catholicism, the new converts kneeled in front of images of Catholic saints, but prayed to African spirits. They borrowed the concept of divine intervention, praying to novena candles, and elaborately dressing graveyard and cathedral altars from the Catholics, but the notion of reverence for nature and one's ancestors comes from Native Americans. Voodoo's rhythmic dances, Congo-inspired music and gumbo-like herb potions came from Africa and Haiti. A famous local musician once told me he thought the hurricanes headed to New Orleans were simply following the paths of slave ships that had arrived three centuries before. If true, voodoo not only survived its origins; its history is deeply rooted with that of New Orleans and of Louisiana.

Tell me, why should it be you have the power to hypnotize me?
Let me live 'neath your spell, Do do that voodoo that you do so well.

—Cole Porter
"You Do Something to Me"

Each year, on June 23rd, on the eve of the birth of St. John the Baptist, celebrated in many ancient cultures as the June solstice, the mark of midsummer, hundreds of voodoo practitioners, residents and tourists alike, gather on the banks of Bayou St. John. There, in Marie Laveau's 'wishing spot,' where she held her first ceremonies, they pay homage to her and to all the ancestors who guide us from beyond.

The author's collection of marble eggs are among her *bricolage*.

To Do Voodoo

Haunted History Voodoo Tours
723 St. Peter Street
(504) 861. 2727

Reverend Zombie's House of Voodoo
725 St. Peter Street
(504) 486. 6366

Voodoo Authentica of New Orleans
Cultural Center and Collection
612 Dumaine Street
(504) 522. 2111

Voodoo Barbecue
1501 St. Charles Avenue
(504) 522. 4647

Voodoo Museum
724 Dumaine Street
(504) 680. 0128

Voodoo Music Experience
City Park
info@thevoodooexperience.com

Voodoux Tattoo
400 S. Jefferson Davis Pkwy
(504) 278. 1465

Soldier, Saint, Sailor, Scribe

I have visited the grand cemeteries of Europe: Paris' Pere Lachaise, Prague's Old Jewish Cemetery and Venice's San Michele. I have passed through the tranquil grounds of Savannah's Bonaventure, nestled off the salty coastal banks of Georgia, and walked the hallowed paths of La Recoleta in Buenos Aires. All have a commonality: limestone and marble angels gather with warriors, soldiers rest next to saints, and headstones bear the names of paupers, poets and politicians.

The Crescent City is home to more than forty cemeteries – ninety percent of which host above-ground mausoleums, due to the city's low water table. At first glance, these 'cities of the dead' resemble small neighborhoods. The rows of weather-pocked stone crypts are often shaped like miniature houses, and are nestled in a straight line, like a small town street, along narrow gravel paths. Grave goers include busloads of tourists, groundskeepers and those who return to mourn and remember. Most, if not all, French Quarter walking tours make a two-block detour to survey St. Louis Cemetery No. 1, while visitors to the Garden District duck into Lafayette Cemetery No. 1 before dining on turtle soup or a bowl of court bouillon at Commander's Palace across the street.

New Orleans cemeteries are beautiful, tranquil, reverent, and somehow European with their etched surnames in Italian, Irish, Spanish, French and German; they are sanctuaries of ritual and rest. Beyond their rusty gates, an air of magic and mystery blows through the city. Perhaps it's the voodoo, or the way life and death (or life and afterlife) mingle so easily here. Jazz funerals give way to raucous parading. Cemetery pilgrimages end with tours of nearby gardens and cathedrals. Eighteenth century buildings reside next to newly-opened cafés. Brief moments coexist, like so many other contradictions in New Orleans, with the here and now. There is no place like it in the world, or the afterworld.

Walking closely behind a brass band, family and friends form a second line in this jazz funeral.

A Graveside Guide:
Symbols Speak for Silent Souls

Pass quietly along the small, silent pathways of the Cities of the Dead. Each tomb, its own intimation on immortality, is topped by stark statuary: a gathering of flowers, crosses, hearts and weeping angels. A sea of undulating symbols speak heavens from beyond the grave. All rise above aged, broken paths of row-upon-row of boxed, barrel-vaulted marble chambers. The astute observer looks closely to glean clues of a life lived here on earth. Behind the carved numerals, in which the passerby subtracts years then months to reveal a life span, and beyond the etched letters alluding to gender and ancestry, a silent language links life to legend.

At first glance, the innocents appear. Children's graves are lovingly marked by long-ago lost lambs, cherubs, and turtle doves. A quiet vernacular hides among the flowers: a daisy for youth and innocence, a lily for a virgin, a calla variety for a departed wife, a morning glory for an absent sibling. There are pansies for remembrance and poppies for eternal sleep. Red roses mark the resting place of a martyred soul; white roses grieve a brief life untouched by events of the ages. Ivy stands for friendship and oak for power; wheat for harvest and a life lived close to the land. Broken tree trunks evoke an early passing and weeping willows whisper eternal sorrow and mourning.

Two horizons merge into one skyline: a cityscape and a city of the dead.

A miniature crypt and a gate with cherubs conjure up heavenly hosts.

Hands tell the tale with an open palm facing upward toward heaven to summon hope. A stronger, masculine hand grasps a severed chain to symbolize the sudden break of life. Gentle fingers intertwine and clasp in prayer pose to symbolize unity and affection beyond the separation of home and hereafter.

Members of the animal kingdom gather among the stone angels and soldiers. Lions symbolize courage and bravery; butterflies signify the metamorphosis of Christ. And here, in a city sandwiched between lake and river, just a few miles north of gulf waters, there is a rare and lone reference to lost sea creatures who have washed upon life's shore. A simple seashell resting atop a parapet or pitched-roof tomb is a loving reminder placed by mere mortals, surviving mourners of the soul departed. Its message: our loved one has left all earthly elements behind to embark upon a spirited journey far, far beyond the grave.

Life is more naked here. You hear smoke stacks and you hear streetcars, faith and death.

— Rick Bragg

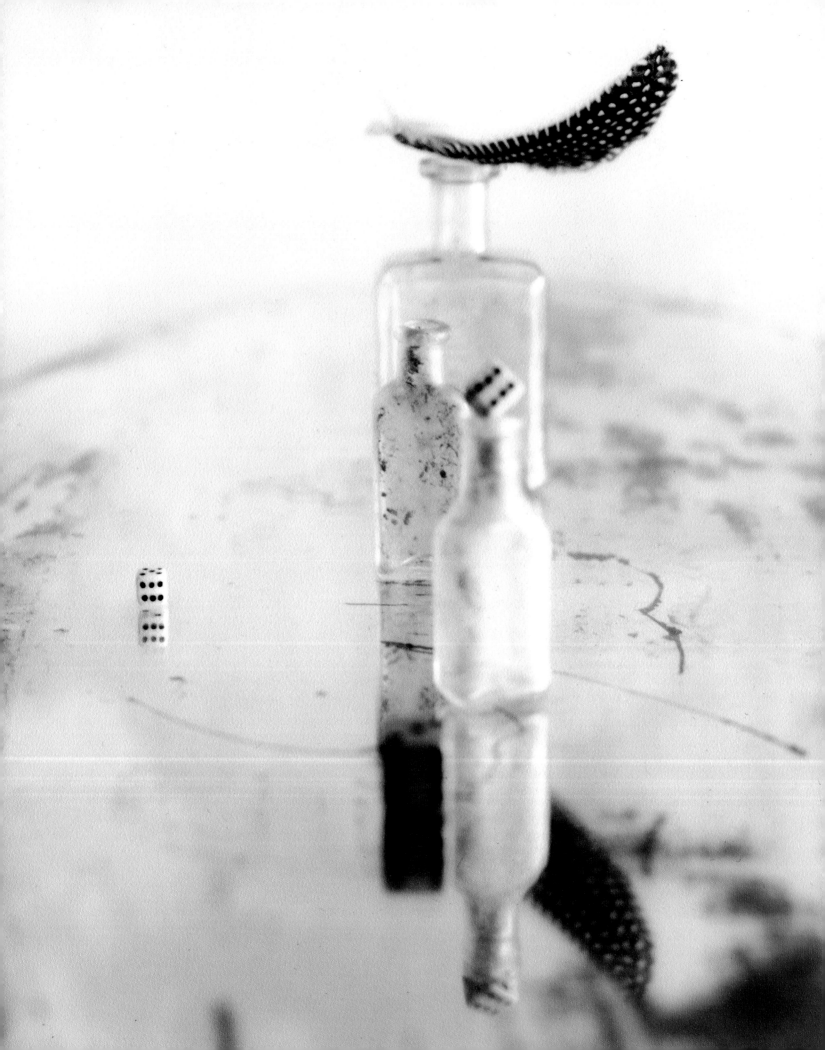

NINE Bottles & Feathers: My Inspirations

I must have known there was a New Orleans house in our future long before we settled on Dumaine Street. Our first road trip as a couple had been to New Orleans. We had both fallen in love with the city separately, and now we fell in love with it all over again, together. It was only fitting that, a few years later, my husband and I returned, just like Scarlett and Rhett before us, for our honeymoon. For the next two-and-a-half decades, we tried, on our parceled-out vacation days, to circle the globe. But through all our years together, and all the miles we traveled, we made sure to keep New Orleans in our orbit.

We loved the lure of new and the embrace of the familiar. We went everywhere, or tried to. We preferred holidays in faraway locales, both European capitals and exotic, unspoiled places like the dense Kalahari deserts of southern Botswana, and the swampy flat jungles of its northern region. We traveled to Monaco and Morocco, Cambodia and Canada, and everywhere in between.

We were amazingly simpatico as travelers, my husband and I, and we almost always agreed on where to go, how long to stay, and what to do once we had arrived. Our itineraries have never included duty-free shops or bargain hunting in department stores; we loved to immerse ourselves in the culture and 'feel' of a place.

Early in our globetrotting, I began collecting all sorts of bric-a-brac, mostly relics of nature, which had little relevance to our New York lives. These treasures of simple found objects, shells, feathers, rocks and beads, came mostly from undiscovered spots, and appealed to me in some primitive way. They lived in boxes that were stored for decades, but were never forgotten. Eventually, they were properly packed up and emigrated from New York to their ultimate resting place on the bookshelves, mantles and tables of our New Orleans home.

Pheasant feathers top a medicine bottle in this photograph by David Halliday.

Beads made of seeds, wood and glass are displayed in the owner's *garçonniére*.

We hand-carried a delicate peacock fan all the way from Thailand. Now, it sits upon the top of a parlor desk next to coarse, sun-bleached cow beads that we'd found in South Africa. Carved Vietnamese prayer beads graced the top of a treasured book. A pair of hollow ostrich eggs from Botswana were first carefully sandwiched between garments in my luggage, and later propped up on each end of the marble fireplace mantle in our upstairs parlor. I arrange Jamaican seashells next to a trio of white Mexican baskets, and topped hand-woven Cambodian chargers with chalky white French *faïencè*. Asian fans rested on the seats of small pink paisley chairs. But long before my finds found their way to the house on Dumaine, I just kept on collecting, kept tucking away these far-flung fragments of our unfolding life together, never really knowing why. Until one day when my friend John came to visit. John, whose ancestors settled in the American South from parts of Africa, eyed my bountiful bricolage and pointed out, with the obvious air of a detective gathering clues, "You have been collecting pieces of the magic."

Of course he was right. These starkly beautiful objects of nature looked their most magical when set against ornate fabrics and beaded pillows. Rich hues and complicated patterns showcased the simplicity of my treasures; plain and fancy together created a grand effect. A style was born in context – and the context was New Orleans. All my seemingly random finds from years of travels past now assumed their rightful places in the house on Dumaine Street. As a result, our house brims with a great mix of cultural keepsakes, becoming a microcosm of New Orleans, herself.

Toile & Talismans

Of all the cultures that have influenced the city, the most intoxicating to me is the heady blend of French and African. In our *garçonniére*, French *toile* hangs next to African ikat, and Kenyan and South African baskets adorn the top of a small Louis XIV table and lit by a French *torchere*. The objects are a playful blend of formal and tribal, of high and low, of nature and handicraft. All seem quite at home in a city that celebrates extremes.

There has always been a balance in New Orleans between the ordinary, and the extraordinary. Take her period architecture: Grand Greek Revival townhouses and Italianate stone pillars are sometimes overshadowed by the simple lines of shotgun houses and Creole cottages. Yet, somehow, everything works together in a blend and flow because, here, style evolves seamlessly. The past lives comfortably with the future. Beauty seems to have no categories or limitations. Everything and everyone seems at home. Old seashells resemble fine sculptures when placed in the proper light, and worn books stacked end-to-end look venerable when turned so that their bindings conceal uneven, deckled pages that peer through worn linen covers. Fine art is often displayed in informal settings. Uptown residents travel downriver to Frenchmen Street for a night of jazz and unceremonious conviviality. Downtowners head upriver for a grander party off St. Charles Avenue near the gilded Garden District.

It has always been so: New Orleans is eternally multi-layered and multi-generational. I see it in its Franco-Spanish-African mix of architecture, music and cuisine. A myriad of world cultures has shaped her: European, African, Caribbean, and American. "Culturally," wrote Walker Percy, "the city is a most peculiar concoction of exotic and American ingredients . . . a gumbo of stray chunks of the South."

Icons and symbols of New Orleans style are repeated, and none is more familiar than the ubiquitous *fleur-de-lis.* The French lily, which was initially embraced as a nod to the city's royal European roots, is now a poignant, ever-present reminder of post-Katrina rebirth. But the city has always been ripe with iconic talismans: Catholic imagery of crosses, Madonna and child, cathedrals and their saints. Only in New Orleans can signs of quiet reverence and raucous revelry co-exist peaceably with no apparent contradiction. There are churches off Bourbon Street and statues of saints stand watch over corner bars.

Portraits of vessels one of pewter, another of porcelain hang on the townhouse walls.

New Orleans is a great city because it nurtures that indefinable essence which drives us to identify ourselves, to delve deep into our souls and discover that thing in life which puts us on an emotional roll. And that emotional roll in turn is the magic which drives us to be ourselves.

—Paul Prudhomme

David Halliday pays tribute to "Bottles and Feathers." *Opposite:* Feathers crown a stack of deckled-edged books.

There is contrast in the Creole hues that brighten the city's Quarter streets. While some are reticent and restrained as the white columns of St. Charles mansions, color blooms like a Watteau garden in varying degrees of intensity everywhere. There are the pastel paint hues of up-town homes, with their stylishly-curated objects and soft silk-and-velvet interiors. Deeper, inside the *Vieux Carré*, brazen Storyville-inspired cafe reds contrast the softer Impressionist hues of the stucco cottages.

At no time is color more alive in New Orleans, more a character in the stage set of her streets, than during Mardi Gras. When Carnival season debuts each year, the city drapes itself in tri-colored swags and sashes. With a palette borrowed from the original colors of the Carnival Krewe Rex – purple for justice, green for faith and gold for power – revelers celebrate with elaborate wax masks, 'throws' of multi-colored beads, and *paper maché* characters that adorn elaborate parade floats.

In New Orleans, the nuances have nuances.

—Wendell Pierce

This is New Orleans: a city proud of its constant contrasts and joyful juxtapositions, sometime fragile, sometimes ethereal, as in the still-life photograph titled, "Bottles and Feathers," by local photographer David Halliday. Here, he tops an array of vintage medicine bottles with delicate quill feathers.

Dainty bottles hold the fragrant tea olive scents
of Hové Parfumeur in the Vieux Carré...

Bartenders arrange their shelves with a
cornucopia of cocktail mixers... Bottles of Lilette
and bitters show off their European-inspired labels.

Mardi Gras Indians choose bright and
fanciful feathered costumes... Magenta feathers
are sewn in a swirled-pattern to form an African
headdress that hangs upon chartreuse-painted walls.

Yards of French-inspired toile whisper
historic tales of the storied Vieux Carré...
of Jackson Square... of St. Louis Cathedral...
and the steamboat Natchez.

New Orleans' interiors wear fine brocades and
Fortuny silks... stripes and harlequin checks...
and velvets the color of clementines.

Crowns are not just for Carnival kings and queens...
they appear on calling cards... and café au lait cups.

Chandeliers glow as beacons everywhere...
in formal parlors and ballrooms...in backroom
bars...and in the reflections of mirrored trumeaus.

Reflective lights shine from bits of mercury glass...
golden gilt and silver...and gas-lit lanterns.

Architectural elements mix columns...
wrought-iron balconies and garden gates...
and courtyards with café chairs.

Nature's fruit is a language all its own...
one of pineapples and hospitality...of kumquats
at Christmas...and the exotica of banana trees
with their flowering purple plants.

There are vessels of every kind...a trio of olive
jars...a silhouetted cup as vase...a pewtered julep
cup nesting the stem of a lily.

Altars appear full with an abundance of angels.

The beating heart of jazz lives here...
and so does Louis Armstrong.

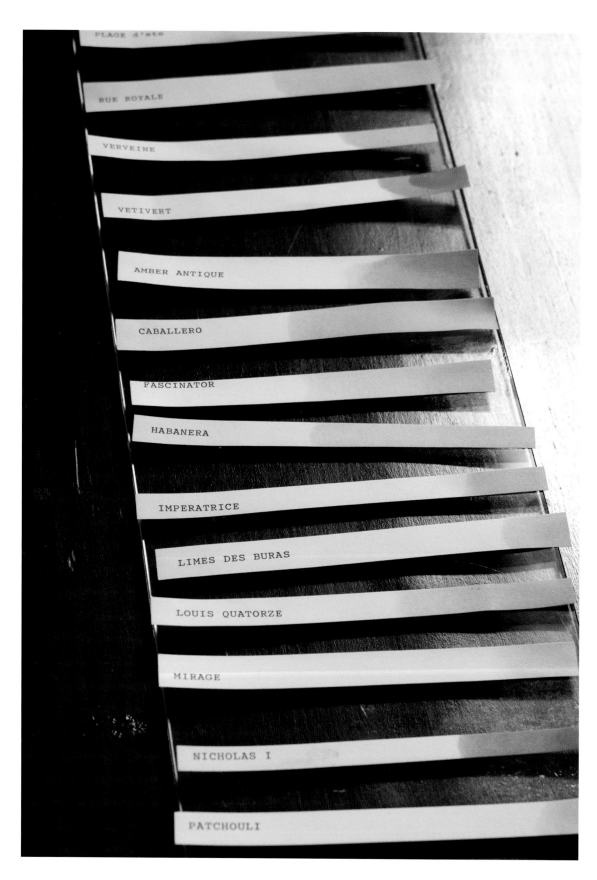

PLAGE d'été

RUE ROYALE

VERVEINE

VETIVERT

AMBER ANTIQUE

CABALLERO

FASCINATOR

HABANERA

IMPERATRICE

LIMES DES BURAS

LOUIS QUATORZE

MIRAGE

NICHOLAS I

PATCHOULI

Scent strips from *Hové* Parfumeur in the *Vieux Carré* are arranged alphabetically. *Opposite:* Chair, book and candle rest along the striped walls of Faulkner House in the *Vieux Carré*.

Lagniappe: My Address Book

New Orleanians are fond of giving the gift of a '*lagniappe*' (lan-yap!) – a Creole word introduced by the Louisiana French, and borrowed from the Spanish phrase 'la napa,' meaning 'something extra.' In his book, *Life on the Mississippi*, Mark Twain declared it "a nice limber, expressive, handy word" and "a word worth travelling to New Orleans to get." Twain was right. Giving a *lagniappe* is yet another ritual that sets New Orleanians apart from their brethren in places like Savannah or Charleston. There, one has to settle for standard acts of Southern hospitality. Here, shopkeepers wrap up a small token as they tally your purchases. A waiter includes an extra *beignet* in the dozen you've just ordered for breakfast. The bartender will most certainly top off your Brandy Alexander with the remains of the shaker, and do so with a smile.

When friends ask for a list of places to eat, or shop, I'd rather give them an experiential *lagniappe*, bypassing the souvenir in favor of a running list of the best oyster dishes, the sounds of a favorite musician performing live on Frenchmen Street, or a shopping list offering only one-of-a-kind items. Following are twelve good reasons to visit the Crescent City, and a dozen more to entice you to come back again.

The French Quarter is what you want it to be.

— George Dureau

Details of a French map appear a century later as a *découpage* tray sold in Hazelnut shop on Magazine Street.

One Fine Day:

What's a perfect day in New Orleans? For me, it's a morning of shopping and antiquing on Magazine Street, followed by an afternoon of art gazing along the galleries lining Camp and Julia streets. Afternoons are spent at the Ogden Museum of Southern Art and the New Orleans Museum of Art and its sculpture garden. As I travel from uptown to the Warehouse District to lakeside, I like to stop for a leisurely lunch in one of the city's small, French-inspired bistros, (Coquette, *2800 Magazine St, (504) 265-0421*, La Petite Grocery, *4238 Magazine St, (504) 891-3377* or Lilette, *3637 Magazine St, (504) 895-1636*).

SHOPS & MUSEUMS:

Hazelnut,
5515 Magazine Street, (504) 891-2424

Scriptura,
5423 Magazine Street, (504) 897-1555

Ann Koerner Antiques,
4021 Magazine Street, (504) 899-2664

Karla Katz Antiques,
4017 Magazine Street, (504)-897-0061

Bremermann Designs,
3943 Magazine Street, (504)-891-7763

Williamson Designs/La Vieille Maison,
3646 Magazine Street, (504) 899-4945

Petricia Thompson Antiques – Shabby Slips,
3522 Magazine Street, (504) 897-5477

Arthur Roger Gallery,
New Orleans Museum of Art,
432 & 434 Julia Street, (504) 658-4100

The Ogden Museum of Southern Art,
University of New Orleans,
925 Camp Street, (504) 539-9600

The New Orleans Museum of Art, City Park,
One Collins Diboll Circle, (504) 658-4100

Two Historic Homes:

Book tours of these two superb houses – both with adjoining gardens.

Longue Vue House & Gardens,
7 Bamboo Road, (504) 488-5488

Pitot House Museum,
1440 Moss Street, (504) 482-0312

Three Flavors of Soup (in one course!):

It's all about the roux! In a city where gumbo and hearty soups reign supreme, leave it to the Brennans, New Orleans' first family of food, to concoct a clever presentation that lets you sample three of the city's best dishes. '1-1-1' includes gumbo, turtle soup and court bouillon, served up in a trio of delicate *demitasse* cups. The dish can be ordered at the better-known Commander's Palace, or my personal favorite, taken at a small table in front of the fireplace at Café Adelaide during winter months. The bartender is always nearby with a dash of sherry for garnishing the turtle soup.

Commander's Palace,
1403 Washington Avenue, (504) 899-8221

Café Adelaide,
300 Poydras Street, (504) 595-3305

Ponchatoula Strawberry Shortcake
at Restaurant August,
301 Tchoupitoulas Street, 504-299-9777

Beignets and Café au Lait at Café du Monde,
800 Decatur Street, (504) 525-4544

Six Sensational 'Sippers':

Pimm's Cup at Café Napoleon,
500 Chartres Street, (504) 524-9752

Ramos Gin Fizz at Commander's Palace,
1403 Washington Avenue, (504) 899-8221

Brandy Milk Punch at Mr. B's Bistro,
201 Royal Street, (504) 523-2078

Sazerac at The Sazerac Bar, The Roosevelt Hotel,
123 Baronne Street, (504) 648-1200

Absinthe at Herbsaint,
701 St. Charles Avenue, (504) 524-4114

Bloody Mary at Cochon,
930 Tchoupitoulas Street, (504) 588-2123

Four Great Places to Rest Your Head:

Even if you're a frugal traveler who bypasses a great
hotel or B&B by rationalizing that little time will be
spent in the room, think again. New Orleans is such a
heady destination, you'll want to include a long bath,
an afternoon nap or a slow-to-rise morning with *café
au lait* and *beignets* to your itinerary.

The Ritz-Carlton Hotel,
921 Canal Street, (504) 524-1331,

The Roosevelt Hotel,
123 Baronne Street, (504) 648-1200

Soniat House,
1133 Chartres Street, (504) 522-0570

Windsor Court,
300 Gravier Street, (504) 523-6000

Seven Shopping Experiences for one-of-a-kind finds:

Aidan Gill,
2026 Magazine Street, (504) 587-9090

Leontine Linens,
3806 Magazine Street, (504) 899-7833

Fleur de Paris,
523 Royal Street, (504) 525-1900

Julie Neill Designs,
3908 Magazine Street, (504) 899-4201

Hazelnut,
5515 Magazine Street, (504) 891-2424

Anne Pratt,
3937 Magazine Street, (504) 891-6532

Nadine Blake,
1036 Royal Street, (504) 529-4913

Five Very Fine Desserts:

Bread Pudding at Mr. B's Bistro,
201 Royal Street, (504) 523-2078

Creole Cream Cheese Cheesecake
at Commander's Palace,
1403 Washington Avenue, (504) 899-8221

Pineapple Upside Down Cake at Cochon,
930 Tchoupitoulas Street, (504) 588-2123

People in hot climates seem to need Spicy food and many festivals.
Who knows why – it's something New Orleans never questions.

— Patrick Dunne

Eight Ways to Enjoy Oysters:

Oyster Rockefeller & Oysters Foch at Antoine's,
713 Saint Louis Street, (504) 581-4422

Fried Oysters on the Half Shell at Mr. B's Bistro,
201 Royal Street, (504) 523-2078

Oyster Loaf at Casamento's,
4330 Magazine Street, (504) 895-9761

P&J Oysters at Restaurant August,
301 Tchoupitoulas Street, (504) 299-9777

Oyster & Bacon Sandwich at Cochon,
930 Tchoupitoulas Street, (504) 588-2123

Oysters St. Claude at Upperline,
1413 Upperline Street, (504) 891-9822

Raw Oysters with a side of Restoration Ale at Felix's,
739 Iberville Street, (504) 522-4440

Nine Books for Your Bookshelf:

*Rising Tide: The Great Mississippi Flood of 1927
and How it Changed America*, by John M. Barry.
(Simon & Schuster)

Nine Lives: Death and Life in New Orleans,
by Dan Baum. (Spiegel & Grau)

Strapless, by Deborah Davis. (Tarcher)

Breach of Faith, by Jed Horne. (Random House)

The Moviegoer, by Walker Percy. (Alfred A. Knopf)

Interview with the Vampire, by Anne Rice.
(Ballantine Books)

Gumbo Tales, by Sara Roahen. (W.W. Norton & Co.)

A Confederacy of Dunces, by John Kennedy Toole.
(Louisiana State University Press)

*Intimate Enemies: The Two Worlds of the
Baroness De Pontalba*, by Christina Vella.
(Louisiana State University Press)

Ten Traveling Tunes:

Walkin' to New Orleans, by Fats Domino.

Do You Know What It Means to Miss New Orleans,
by Louis Armstrong.

In the Upper Room, by Mahalia Jackson.

Tipitina, by Professor Longhair.

Such a Night, by Dr. John.

Hey, Pocky-way, by The Neville Brothers.

My Feet Can't Fail Me Now,
by Dirty Dozen Brass Band.

Zydeco Boogaloo, by Buckwheat Zydeco.

Jungle Blues, by Wynton Marsalis.

Just a Closer Walk With Thee, by Dr. Michael White.

Eleven Great Tastes:

Muffuletta at Central Grocery,
923 Decatur Street, (504) 523-1620

Roast Beef Po' Boy at Parkway Bakery,
538 Hagan Street, (504) 482-3047

Praline Bacon at Elizabeth's,
601 Gallier Street, (504) 944-9272

Crabmeat Maison at Galatoire's,
209 Bourbon Street, (504) 525-2021

Slow-roasted Duck at Brigtsen's,
723 Dante Street, (504) 861-7610

Crawfish Étouffée at K-Paul's,
416 Chartres Street, (504) 524-7394

Seafood Gumbo at Stanley,
1031 Decatur Street, (504) 593-0006

Cochon du Lait (or Catfish Court Bouillon) at Cochon,
930 Tchoupitoulas Street, (504) 588-2123

Cane River Country Shrimp at Upperline,
1413 Upperline Street, (504) 891-9822

Andouille Sausage at Emeril's,
800 Tchoupitoulas Street, (504) 528-9393

Shrimp Mosca at Mosca's,
*4137 Highway 90 W, Westwego, LA,
(504) 436-8950*

Twelve reasons to return to New Orleans again and again...

Carnival & Mardi Gras *(February)*.
Tennessee Williams Festival *(March)*.
Stella & Stanley Shouting Contest *(March)*.
French Quarter Festival *(April)*.
New Orleans Jazz & Heritage Festival *(April/May)*.
Creole Tomato Festival *(June)*.
Tales of the Cocktail *(July)*.
The Essence Music Festival *(July)*.
Satchmo Summerfest *(July/August)*.
White Linen Night (August).
Dirty Linen Night (August).
Words & Music Festival (November).

AFTERWORD *The Second Line*

In keeping with a beloved New Orleans tradition, I have saved the 'second line' for last.

There are more parades through the streets of New Orleans than there are traffic stop lights in any mid-size American city. They often begin with a single blaring trumpet blast, almost biblical and Gabriel-like in its rallying cry, and always follow with a processional behind a traditional brass band. Bystanders call it a parade. Participants know it as a second line. Followers dance and gambol in pied-piper fashion, sometimes through traffic, while swinging napkins, handkerchiefs or another make-shift 'do rag' overhead, as they snake behind a tuba or the slide trombone. The brass bands, which thankfully number almost forty today, are often made up of young and old members, all multi-generations of one of the city's social aid and pleasure clubs.

> *New Orleanians have long memories and a high tolerance for eccentricity.*
>
> —Randy Fertel

A long-held tradition from the late 1940's, the second line might be a funeral (locals call them 'jazz funerals'), a wedding, a birthday, or another occasion. The ultimate jazz funeral begins with a slow, somber 'walk with thee' before gathering mourners change rhythm ending in a high-step dance leading the deceased into a final 'moment of glory' and toward their 'eventual resting place.' Second liners don't always know the deceased or the reason at hand; followers know to simply step in line.

Here's to my very own second line – all those who gladly followed me on the journey that eventually led to this book.

Fancy footwork from a second line stops the parade.

Street music is most prevalent in the strains of the jazz funeral and the sounds of the city's ubiquitous brass bands. *Opposite:* Funeral followers take "a closer walk with thee."

First, to three special men in my life: to my husband Jerry, who believed in the city enough to buy a house just weeks following the devastating levee breaks of Katrina; to my dear friend, Michael Clinton, who pleaded with me to write about my love affair with New Orleans; and to dearest Hal Williamson, who literally transformed our French Quarter house into a home.

To those artists and photographers who shared their love of the Crescent City through vivid images: Simon Blake, Karena Cawthon, Patrick Cicalo, Jocelyn Cole, Rod Cook, Steven Forster, Jennifer Gordon, David Halliday, John Kernick, Raymond Meeks, Ericka Molleck Goldring, Landon Nordeman, Alexa Pulitzer, Lauren Rieth, Josephine Sacabo, Richard Sexton, Susan Sully and David Tompkins. Special thanks to Maura McEvoy, who returned to a more vibrant city to capture its beauty three years after our first trip to chronicle the devastation of the levee breaks after Katrina.

To those who helped with the words: Ella Brennan, Emeril Lagasse, Wynton Marsalis and George and Wendy Rodrigue; and with content: Michele Bernhardt, Nadine Blake, Joel Dondis, Michael Fielding, Michael Harold, Jane Scott Hodges, Pam Janis, Bethany Lewis, Wendy Lyn, George Massey, Quinn Peeper, Sherry Potten, Amanda Talley, Teri Troncale, Hal Williamson and Louis Wilson. Special thanks to Mary Randolph Carter, a Southern sister whose first book inspired my own. And of course, to Marta Hallett, my amazing publisher (thank you for your "instant" yes), and to Sarah Morgan Karp for translating the images of dozens of artists into a seamless, beautiful book.

And finally, to both the natives and the newly arrived, the tourists and the volunteers, and all the fellow wayfarers, who like me, embrace every sidewalk crack and flowering magnolia in our beloved city of *La Nouvelle Orleans*.

My New Orleans by
Debra Shriver

Occupation: Publicist, author, media executive.

The best thing about the city is: the irrepressible spirit & _joie de vivré_ of its people.

My favorite meal is: any dish topped with oysters.

My favorite cocktail is: a Pimm's Cup.

New Orleans is the only place in the world where: people dance in the street on a daily basis.

My favorite neighborhood is: the _Vieux Carré_, a walker's paradise.

The city's most marked characteristics are: a love of good food and good times.

My favorite New Orleanian is: all the musicians who march in the city's brass bands.

If I had a free hour, I would spend it: sitting in my courtyard.

My one New Orleans obsession is: the Mardi Gras Indians.

I knew the spell of the city had been cast upon me when: I found the house of my dreams.

The marquee lights of Armstrong Park proudly announce the city's devotion to its favorite son.

GLOSSARY

Banquette [ban'ket] noun / French word still used for sidewalk or a small bank along the road.

Bayou [by'you] noun / Slow, shallow stream running through a marsh or swampy area.

Beignets [ben yeah] noun / French word for fritters or fried doughnuts.

Big Easy [big ee-zee] noun / A colloquial name for New Orleans; an early 1900's musician reference to finding easy work in a place with few alcohol restrictions.

Boudin [boo-dan] noun / Hot, spicy pork sausage stuffed with rice, onions and herbs.

Café Brulot [caf-fay broo-lih] noun / Brew of hot coffee, orange peel and other spices, and liqueurs blended in a chafing dish, ignited and served following the dessert course.

Cajun [ka-jen] noun / A Louisianian descended from French-speaking Acadian immigrants; relating to, or prepared in a style of cooking originating among the Cajuns and characterized by the use of hot seasonings (i.e., cayenne pepper).

Cher [sheR] pronoun / An endearing greeting used for loved one.

Chicory [chick or e] noun / Bitter root plant from the endive family, which is roasted and ground for use in coffee blends.

Creole [cree-ol] adjective / Descendant of New Orleans' original French and Spanish settlers.

Dressed [drest] adjective / Used to describe sandwich or po' boy served with lettuce, tomatoes and mayonnaise.

Étoufée [ay-too-FAY] noun / A French word meaning 'to smother'; a spicy Cajun stew made with crawfish, sauteed vegetables and a dark roux or gravy, and served over rice.

Fais Do-Do [fay doh-doh] noun / Cajun French phrase for 'go to sleep'; a communal dance where children were put to bed at the dance.

Faubourg [Fo-berg] noun / Another word for suburb or neighborhood.

Filé [Fe-la] noun / Powder made from dried sassafras leaves – first made by Louisiana's Choctaw Indians in thickening gumbo or for medicinal purposes.

Flambé [Flam-bay] adjective / Culinary term meaning served with flaming liquor.

Garçonniére [gr son-yer] noun / A bachelor's apartment or rear studio of a residence.

Go Cup [goh kuhp] noun / A disposable cup for consumption of alcoholic beverages consumed on the street, or in transit where open glass containers are illegal.

Grilllades [gri-lahdz] noun / Browned steak or veal cooked in a tomato gravy.

Gris-Gris [gree-gree] noun / A voodoo spell sometimes used for evil purposes; also a small bag or charm worn around the neck to ward off negative spirits.

Gumbo [guhm-boh] noun / A rich, aromatic Creole soup or stew usually made with tomatoes, okra, meats, vegetables & file powder.

Jambalaya [jom'ba-LIE-a] noun / A meat or seafood dish, sautéed and served over rice.

Lagniappe [lan-yap] noun / An extra or unexpected gift or benefit; a bonus.

Laissez les bons temps roulez! [le-say le bon-ton rou-la] verb / A favorite Cajun French expression meaning, "Let the good times roll."

Maque Choux [mock shoe] noun / A Cajun corn and vegetable sauté.

Makin' groceries [mey-kin groh-suh-ries] verb / Buying groceries.

Mardi Gras [marty-graw] noun / (Shrove Tuesday) – French for 'Fat Tuesday;' the day of feasting before Ash Wednesday, the first day of Lent.

Mojo [moh-joh] noun / A magic spell, hex or charm.

Muffuletta [Muff-a-LOT-a] noun / A quintessential New Orleans Italian sandwich of ham, Genoa salami, mortadella, Provolone cheese and marinated olive salad on a round seeded Italian loaf; first served at Central Grocery on Decatur Street in the French Quarter.

Neutral Ground [noo-truhl grahynd] noun / Grassy median between the paved lanes of a boulevard.

Picayune [Pic'ee yoon] noun / Meaning small or small-minded (a Spanish coin worth approximately six cents); the city's daily newspaper, the New Orleans *Times-Picayune*.

Praline [PRAH-leen] noun / Common Creole candy made from pecans and sugar (or coconut and sugar).

Po' Boy [POE-boy] noun / Quintessential New Orleans sandwich of meat or seafood served on French bread.

Remoulade [REM oo Lad] noun / A sauce of spices and seasonings used as a marinade for boiled shrimp; served as an appetizer.

Roux [ru] noun / Basic mixture of flour and butter or flour and shortening for sauces, gravies and soups.

Second Line [sek-uhnd lahyn] noun / A group of revelers traditionally sporting umbrellas & handkerchiefs that trails the band (which is the fist line) in New Orleans' parades; a line following mourners at a traditional jazz funeral.

Vieux Carré [voo-ca-ray] noun / French term for 'old square,' commonly used to designate New Orleans' French Quarter.

Voodoo [voo-doo] noun / A religious tradition first brought by African slaves and based on the appreciation of ancestors and nature.

Yat [yat] verb / Colloquial greeting meaning "Where yat?" or "hello, how are you doing?"

Zydeco [zi-di-ko] noun / Popular music of southern Louisiana that combines French dance melodies, elements of Caribbean music, and the blues, played by small groups featuring the guitar, the accordion, and a washboard.

BIBLIOGRAPHY

Website References

Antique, China, Porcelain & Collectibles
www.antique-china-porcelain-collectibles.com

City of New Orleans
www.cityofno.com

Discover France
www.discoverfrance.com

Gourmet Sleuth
www.gourmetsleuth.com

Leontine Linens
www.leontinelinens.com

Lexicon of New Orleans
Terminology and Speech
www.gumbopages.com

Lucky Mojo
www.luckymojo.com

Napoleon House
www.napoleonhouse.com

New Orleans Cemeteries
www.nolacemeteries.com

New Orleans Online
www.neworleansonline.com

New York Social Diary
www.newyorksocialdiary.com

Old and Sold
www.oldandsold.com

Visual Vamp
www.visualvamp.blogspot.com

Wikipedia
www.wikipedia.org

People Referenced

Bernhardt, Michele
Hodges, Jane Scott
Kelley, Brandi C.
Pulitzer, Alexa
Sully, Susan
Sustendal, Diane
Williamson, Hal

Articles

Broom, Sarah, "A Closer Walk With Thee,"
New York Times Magazine, January 22, 2006.

Bullard, E. John, "Rodrigue's Louisiana: Cajuns,
Blue Dogs and Beyond Katrina," *Arts Quarterly*,
Jan/Feb/March 2008.

Knight, Rebecca, "My Version of Jerusalem,"
Financial Times, May 16/17, 2009.

Cushner, Susie, "Something About Silhouettes,"
Country Living, January 2009.

Delehanty, Randolph, "On Our Bookshelf,"
Victoria, January/February 2009.

Dennen, Richard, "Southern Belle,"
Tatler, July 2009.

Dunne, Patrick, "Elegant Evolution,"
Southern Accents, March/April 2009.

Harris, Jessica, "Open City," *Saveur*, No.115.

Huber, Leonard V., *New Orleans: A Pictorial
History*, Pelican Publishing Company, 1991.

Huber, Leonard V., *Creole Collage*,
Center for Louisiana Studies, 1980.

Keefe, John W., "The Porcelains of Paris, 1770-1870," *Magazine Antiques*, February 1996.

Lewis, Michael, "Wading Toward Home," *New York Times*, October 9, 2005.

Marshall, Alex, "The Extreme Boulevardier," *New York Times*, August 19, 2007.

Martinez, Jill, "A Journey Down St. Charles Ave." *Louisiana Homes & Gardens*, January 2009.

Matalin, Mary, "Everywhere I go There are Church Bells," *Financial Times*, May 23/24, 2009.

Mullener, Elizabeth, "The Queen of Cuisine," *Times-Picayune*, October 7, 2007.

Packard, Morgan, "The Gumbo of Vodou," *New Orleans Magazine*, June 2009.

Percy, Walker, "New Orleans Mon Amour," *Harper's Magazine*, September 1968.

Read, Mimi, "Trying to Leave New Orleans Blues," *House Beautiful*, May 1992.

Read, Mimi, "A Match for Lucullus," *Southern Accents*, November 1993.

Reed, Julia, "The Soul of New Orleans," *Garden and Gun*, December 2008/January 2009.

Shriver, Jerry, "Delicious Food Fight Embroils New Orleans," *USA Today*, August 1, 2002.

"What is Jazz," *Daily News*, April 21, 2009.

Television

"American Experience," PBS Transcript, February 12, 2007.

IMAGE CREDITS

With thanks to the artists, all images, including front and back jacket, are copyright © Maura McEvoy, except those which are copyright © on the pages as follows:

Simon Blake: 66, 67, 88, 89, 93, 97, 98, 102, 107, 170, 171, 176, 177, 179;

Karena Cawthon: 50, 65, 81, 139, 152;

Patrick Cicalo: 24-25;

Jocelyn Cole: 120;

Rod Cook: 65;

Jennifer Gordon: 140, 141;

David Halliday: 5, 26, 30, 31, 33, 34, 35, 39, 40, 41, 87, 106, 142, 162, 166, 167, 168, 179;

John Kernick: 5, 7, 52, 57, 58, 68, 71, 86;

Raymond Meeks: 32, 37, 64;

Ericka Molleck Goldring: 19, 20, 21, 22, 130, 156, 180, 182, 183, 184-185;

Landon Nordemann: 108-109, 110, 119;

George Rodrique: 5, 8, 11;

Josephine Sacabo: 29, 38;

Richard Sexton: 6, 46, 116, 121, 133, 146, 148, 149, 151, 152, 159, 160, 161;

Courtesy of Soniat House: 42, 45, 47, 177;

Susan Sully: 49, 57, 60, 61, 62, 68, 170;

David Tompkins: 5, 23, 107.

INDEX